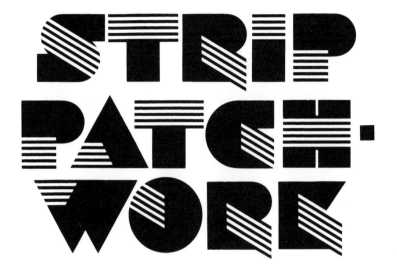

STRIP PATCHWORK

Valerie Campbell-Harding

Dover Publications, Inc., New York

Library of Congress Cataloging-in-Publication Data

Campbell-Harding, Valerie.
    Strip patchwork / Valerie Campbell-Harding
        p.   cm.
    Reprint. Originally published: London : B.T. Batsford, 1983.
    Bibliography: p.
    Includes index.
    ISBN 0–486–25729–0
    1. Patchwork—Patterns.   I. Title.   II. Title: Strip patchwork.
TT835.C357 1988
746.46—dc19   87–33087
                                                              CIP

Printed in Great Britain

Contents

Acknowledgment

I should like to thank Deirdre Amsden, Sarah Balmain, Janice Hay, Elizabeth Heitzmann, Daphne Nicholson, Anne Ohlenschlager, Clare Paterson, Yvonne Pedretti, Margaret Rivers, Helen Robertson, Pamela Watts and Sheila Wells for allowing me to photograph their work; also Eunice Wells for making some items for me, and Daphne Nicholson for allowing me to include one of her designs. Thanks also to Vincent Morris for printing my photographs so superbly. Lastly, a very special thank you to Andrea Statham for her help, support and advice, and for allowing me to use photographs of her work.

Valerie Campbell-Harding
Vernham Dean, 1983

Definitions

These terms are used throughout the book:

Block   A shape, usually a square, made by sewing a number of pieces of fabric together. The blocks are usually sewn together to make a repeat pattern. Blocks can be triangular, hexagonal or parallelograms, or any shape that will fit with the next and leave no spaces between.

Patch   A single piece of fabric cut to any shape required by the design.

To piece   The seaming together of pieces of fabric to make a larger pattern.

Pre-stripped fabric   Strips of fabric sewn together to make a larger area.

Template   A shape made of card, plastic or metal, used as a pattern for cutting strips or shapes from fabric.

The makers of the patchwork items illustrated are given in italics at the end of the captions. All the photographs except numbers 4, 6 and 100 were taken by the author. The drawings are also by the author.

6

Introduction: Design Ideas and Sources

Strip patchwork is usually the name given to the craft of cutting long strips of fabric of various widths and colours and sewing them together by machine to make a new fabric. However, this book also covers other design and sewing methods for patchwork which includes strips.

Pre-stripped fabric can be cut across the seams and the strips re-assembled in a different order to make simple or intricate patterns more quickly than would be possible by sewing each individual shape to its neighbour. Shapes such as triangles, diamonds or curves can be cut from the stripped fabric, and sewn together into a pattern as in block patchwork. Strips of fabric can be sewn to a backing fabric to give added body and firmness and to avoid creasing. Texture can be added by quilting the patchwork, by making pleats and tucks, or by inserting flaps or turned shapes into the seams. The seams can be on the right side of the work and the edges frayed.

Colour and tone are extremely important ingredients in patchwork and therefore a section on dyeing has been included so that your designs can be carried out exactly as they were envisaged.

There are so many sewing methods for joining strips of fabric together to make patchwork that they have been combined in a section of their own. Many of the designs can be made up using more than one of the methods, so it seemed sensible to keep the instructions in one place. Names for these methods vary, and some have no names – log cabin patchwork seems to be the only name that is widely used for a particular pattern, so this is the only one that I have used.

I have tried to suggest design *methods* rather than just to give finished designs, as it is always possible when following a method to introduce your own vartiations to give individuality to the work. Indeed you *should* vary the method as much as possible. Satisfaction comes from having designed your own patchwork, as well as from making it. The following pages suggest many sources of design.

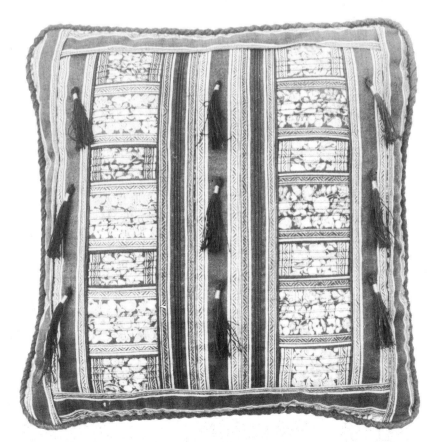

1 Cushion made from strips of a patterned fabric, using both the back and the front of the fabric. Pin tucks are put in to give added texture and folds of plain colour are included at the edges of the strips. (*Valerie Campbell-Harding*)

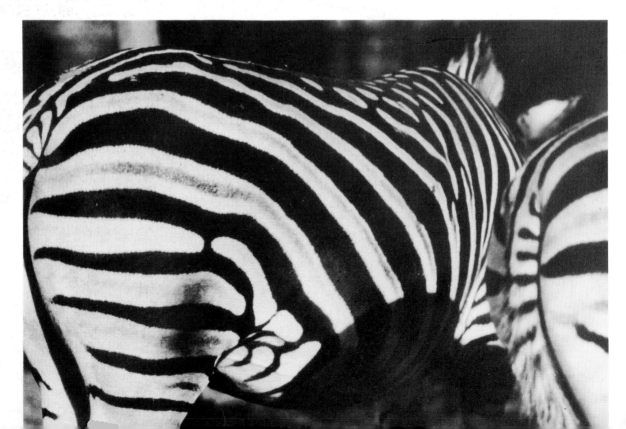

2, 3 *Left* Ideas for designs using stripes are everywhere, and can be photographed even with a very simple camera. If you are worried about your drawing ability, then your photographs can be traced and used in one of the ways suggested later (page 35). Looking at the environment helps you to notice subtleties of angle, curve and width which can be incorporated into designs

4 An aerial view of terraced crops. The light strips are lying fallow and the dark ones are growing wheat. All or part of this picture could be used as a design or areas could be taken from it. The variations in the widths of the strips make the contrast between foreground and distant parts more definite, and the curved shapes are a focal point. You might wish to alter the placing of some parts of the pattern. This illustration was taken from a photocopy of a photograph, a useful technique for clarifying and simplifying a design

9

10

5 *Left* Two photocopies of drinking straws. One was made with the straws laid on the machine and the copy taken with the lid closed. The second copy was made with the lid open. The photocopies were cut into 2.5 cm (1 in.) strips and woven. It is the counterbalance of black on white and white on black which is interesting, and also the spaces between the straws. Each square is slightly different from all the others

6 The reflection of another building in this window is made even more interesting by the distortion caused by uneven glass. The combination of straight and curved lines is effective, and the whole pattern is held together by the metal grid

7 Stacked chairs outside a French restaurant. The curves would not be difficult to sew, and the combination of curves, straight lines and small square hollows on the chair legs would combine to make interesting patchwork

8 *Right* A piece of striped fabric was placed on a photocopying machine and pressed down while being processed. A tracing of parts of the pattern could be made and enlarged to make a strip design. The combination of wide and narrow lines and the many different angles is exciting, as is the tonal contrast. This could be the basis of a design for a whole quilt, or parts of it could be used for a smaller article or border

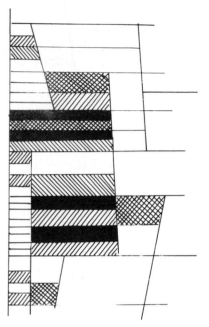

9 Ideas can come from unlikely sources, such as this child's game with card squares patterned in black and white. There are other patterns in the box and they could be put together to make many different designs, straight or curved

11, 12 Drawings based on sections of Paul Klee paintings, showing an interesting variation in the width of the stripes, and a contrast between large empty spaces and small detailed areas

10 A painting by Bridget Riley has been adapted for patchwork by adding a central line. The original is in black and white, but there is an opportunity for using colour or tonal progressions; for example, you could work from red through shades of purple to blues, or from dark colours at the bottom to light shades at the top

13 This is a college dormitory and shows how short, straight lines can suggest curves. The variation in stripe widths is interesting and, together with the change of length, suggests depth. I also like the contrast between the hard lines of the ceiling and panelling and the soft stripes of the curtains

Proportion

The relative proportions of the various widths of the strips in patchwork are vitally important and should be carefully thought out to produce a satisfying result.

The simplest method is to have the strips of equal width. For some designs this is quite sufficient, particularly if the patchwork is going to be cut up and re-sewn. However there are times when you will want a more interesting and intricate pattern, and the easiest way to decide on the width of the strips is to think up a series of numbers (any numbers) and repeat them. For example, use 1, 2 and 3. Decide on a width which will represent one unit – the units can range in width from 6 mm (¼ in.) to as large as you wish. '2' will

represent two units, '3' three units and so on. The units can follow any sequence, such as 1-2-3-1-2-3, or 1-2-3-2-1, or 1-2-3-3-2-1. Almost any combination will be successful if it is repeated often enough. The following diagrams show strip patterns using number sequences, with not more than four numbers in each one.

14

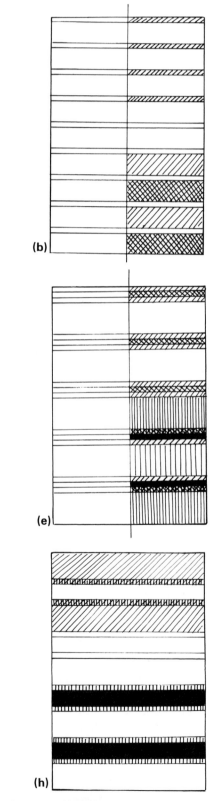

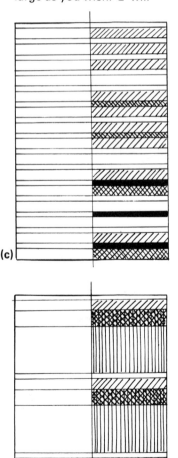

(a)

(b)

(c)

(d)

(e)

(f)

(g)

(h)

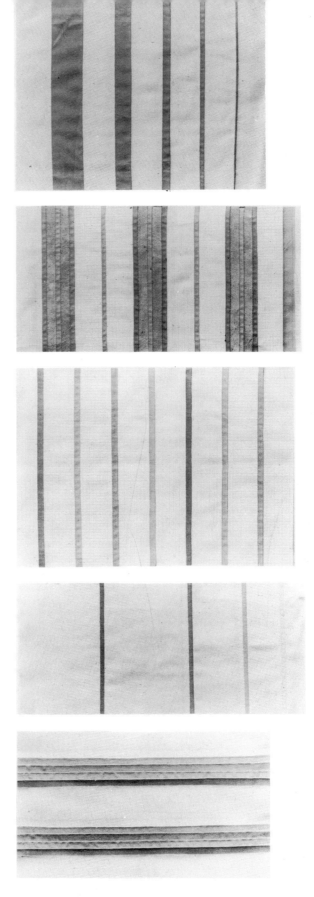

14 *Left* (a) The stripes are of equal width (2-2-2- etc)
(b) Using 1 and 4 alternately (1-4-1-4 etc)
(c) 1-2-1-2
(d) 1-1-4-1-1-4
(e) 1-1-1-6-1-1-1-6
(f) 1-2-3-9-1-2-3-9
(g) 2-1-2-6-2-1-2-6
(h) 1-3-1-5-1-3-1-5

15 Pieced samples using combinations of numbers similar to those on the previous page to establish the proportion of coloured strips to the cream background strips. Any or all of these can be used in one piece of work, if the colours are related. For ways of doing this, look in folk museums at the clothes of the Guatemalan Indians, who make garments of woven striped fabrics with many different materials worn together. The secret is to keep to a restricted colour scheme

16 Four cushions showing
interesting proportions of stripes,
and also of striped to plain areas.
Notice the placing of tabs, which
sometimes carries the pattern
through to the edge of the cushion,
and sometimes shifts it. (*Andrea
Statham*)

The Fibonacci series
Leonardo Fibonacci, an early thirteenth-century mathematician, arrived at a series of numbers in which each number is the sum of the previous two. This series turned out to be in the same ratio as many proportions of growth found in nature, such as the spiral of seeds in the centre of a sunflower or pine cone, or the markings on a shell. The ratio of the various parts of the body to each other follows this series, and so does the division of stems and branches of plants and trees.

This is the series:

0 + 1 = 1
1 + 1 = 2
1 + 2 = 3
2 + 3 = 5
3 + 5 = 8
5 + 8 = 13
8 + 13 = 21 and so on

Figure 17 shows the series translated into stripes.

If you base the proportion of your stripes on any part of the series it will look 'right'. You can also adapt the basic proportions to make more intricate patterns with the series, going in two, three or four directions. It is very difficult to sew strips less than 6 mm (¼ in.) wide, so if you make the basic unit 6 mm, then the width of the strips would be: 6 mm, 12 mm, 18 mm, 30 mm, 48 mm, 78 mm and 126 mm, or ¼ in., ½ in., ¾ in., 1¼., 2 in., 3¼ in. and 5¼ in., if you are using the imperial system. This can be enlarged as much as you wish.

When designing with cut paper, you can cut the strips exactly this size, but do not forget to add a seam allowance when cutting strips from fabric. If you find that the numbers get too unwieldy, which they do very quickly, start adding them together as soon as you reach double figures, leaving out any 0s. This is called the reduced Fibonacci series and

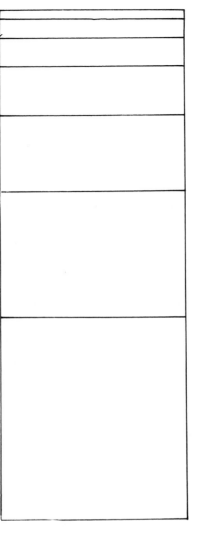

17 Fibonacci series

goes like this:

0 + 1 = 1
1 + 1 = 2
1 + 2 = 3
2 + 3 = 5
3 + 5 = 8
5 + 8 = 4 (13 = 1 + 3)
8 + 13 = 3 (21 = 2 + 1)
13+ 21 = 7 (34 = 2 = 4)
21 + 34 = 1 (55 = 5 + 5) and so on

Much use of this reduced series was made by the Arabs, with whom Fibonacci studied, and it is incorporated into many of their intricate geometric designs.

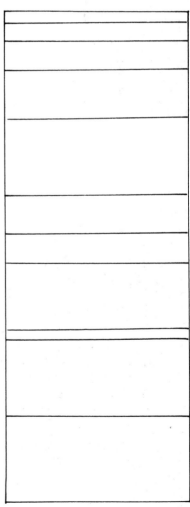

18 Reduced Fibonacci series

19-20 Designing using the Fibonacci series. Photocopies of fabric were cut into strips following the series (1-2-3-5-8). A sheet of plain-coloured paper was cut in the same way. Both papers were glued to another sheet of paper, placed in opposite sequence

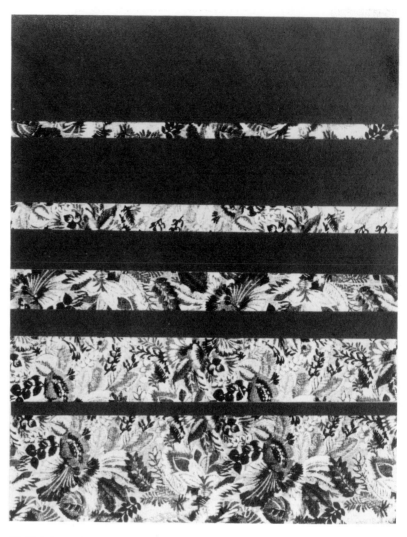

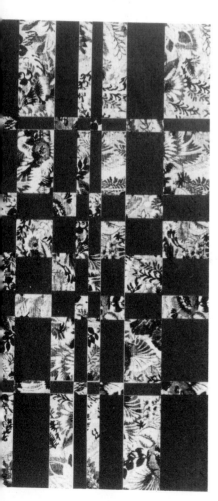

19 This is the first design, and is reminiscent of a garden seen through a Venetian blind

20 The first design was cut in the opposite direction, using the same series. Alternate strips were reversed to give a more intricate pattern. Any design planned like this with paper can be sewn with fabric, but do not forget to add seam allowances on both sides of the strips

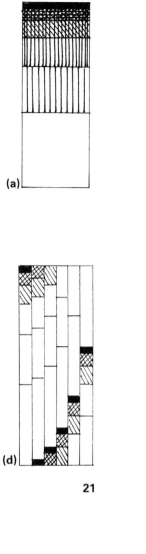

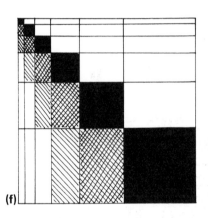

(a)

(b)

(c)

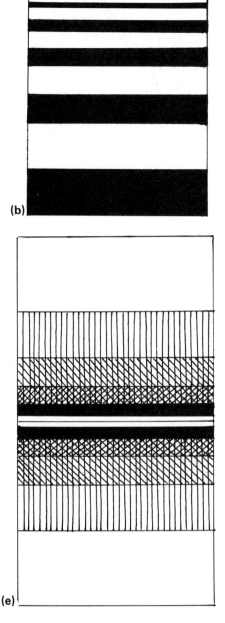

21

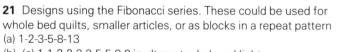

(d)

(f)

(e)

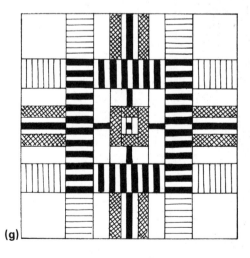

(g)

21 Designs using the Fibonacci series. These could be used for whole bed quilts, smaller articles, or as blocks in a repeat pattern
(a) 1-2-3-5-8-13
(b), (c) 1-1-2-2-3-3-5-5-8-8 in alternate dark and light
(d) The same sequence as (a), cut up and shifted to give the impression of a curve
(e) The same sequence used in two directions: 13-8-5-3-2-1-1-2-3-5-8-13
(f) The sequence again used in two directions, but starting at the top and working downwards, and at the left-hand edge and working towards the right
(g) The Fibonacci series in four directions. From the left into the centre and out again to the right; and from the top to the centre and out again to the bottom

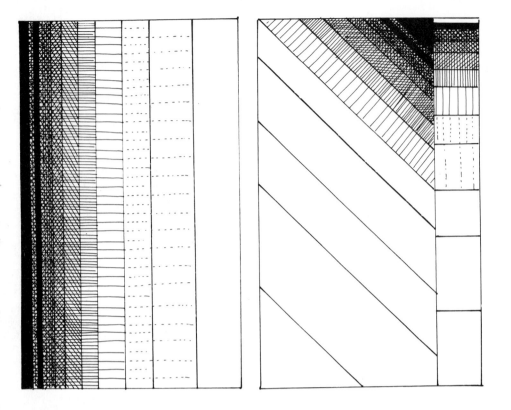

22 Designs using the Fibonacci series. Each number is repeated twice in the horizontal stripes, and once in the diagonal stripes. The pieced seams could be continued into a plain border with lines of quilting stitches. Borders can be added following the same sequence outwards, and detail can be included in some areas (see page 118)

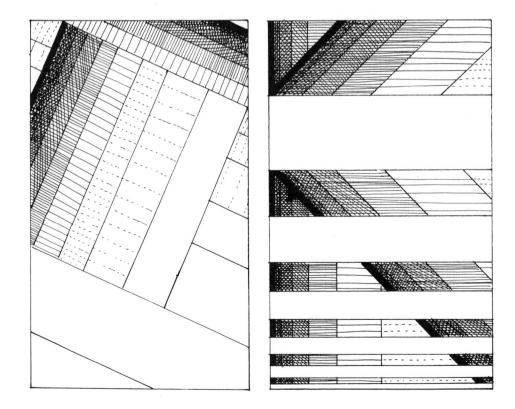

Dyeing

When you have tramped the streets for days searching in vain for a fabric in a particular colour, you begin to think of dyeing your own fabrics. With a little experience you can reproduce exactly any colour that you have dyed, even after an interval of months or years. You can gradually build up a good stock of dyed fabrics so that any new design can be made up in exactly the colours you want without having to wait for a dyeing session. Also, you are not restricted to using the colours which happen to be fashionable in a particular year. At the same time as you dye the fabric, dye some yarns for cords and tassels. There are some dyeing methods that give patterned or textured fabrics which cannot be bought. Space-dyeing produces a multi-coloured effect on one piece of fabric or along a length of yarn. Patterned fabrics can be over-dyed in a stronger colour to unify a mixed bundle of patterns, or to subdue a pattern which is too

strong. Suddenly some of the fabrics that you have had for years and never been able to use become just the thing at very little cost.

Dyes
Many people only use natural dyes, but most of these are not very good on cotton or silk without a mordant, which can be a nuisance to use. However, my main reason for not using natural dyes is that the colours cannot be repeated exactly, as they vary from week to week, even within a season. With chemical dyes you can get bright or subtle colours and can repeat them exactly. They do not have quite the interesting depth of colour of natural dyes, but in a piece of patchwork this is hardly noticeable. So, the most useful dyes for the home dyer are the direct dyes (hot-water), the fibre-reactive dyes (cold-water) and some natural dyes such as indigo, tea, onion skins and certain spices

(also hot-water). Chemical dyes are easily obtainable in small tins, and suppliers for dyes in larger quantities are listed at the end of the book (page 143).

Direct dyes
These are very fast to light, but bleed when washed, and go on bleeding. Articles made from fabric dyed with these should be dry-cleaned. You can get lovely dark colours, as well as medium and pale ones, and they are simple to use.

Fibre-reactive dyes
These are extremely fast to light and washing, as the dye reacts with the molecules of the fibres. They are easier for experimenting with than the hot-water dyes and can be sprayed, painted, dabbed or dripped onto the fabric.

Both these types of dye are good with cotton, silk, linen and rayon. The direct dyes also work well with wool and nylon.

Equipment

You will need kitchen scales, a measuring jug, measuring spoons, jam jars, a stick for stirring (a dowelling rod painted with three coats of polyurethane varnish is ideal), an overall, rubber gloves, a timer, a plastic bucket for cold-water dyeing and an old jam pan for hot-water dyeing. When you begin dyeing, use the small tins that can be bought anywhere. Later on you will find that it is more economical to buy dye in larger quantities.

Preparation

All fabrics and threads should be well washed before you attempt to dye them. Cottons can be put through the appropriate cycle in the washing machine, but silk and wool should be gently washed by hand. Unbleached calico needs sterner treatment and should be soaked for at least ten minutes, then washed at the hottest cycle. Next boil the calico for half an hour with half a cup of washing soda, rinse and dry it. I do this in 5.5 metre (6 yard) lengths as that quantity just fits my washing machine and boiler. It is worth keeping a supply of washed fabrics and yarns so that when the urge to dye comes upon you, you can give in to it without delay. All yarns should be tied in skeins, then gently washed by hand to avoid tangling.

All fabrics, dye powder, water and solutions should be accurately weighed or measured every time, so that you can repeat the results. Keep a file with the recipes and samples, as it is impossible to remember exactly what you have done. Make the salt and soda solutions in large quantities and keep them in plastic or glass bottles. They will keep indefinitely. It is much easier to use these solutions than to have to mix dry crystals every time.

Salt solution
Salt drives the colour into the fibres. Mix 250 gm (9 oz) of cooking salt with hot water to make 1 litre (1¾ pints) of solution. Stir until the salt is dissolved, and pour into the container.

Soda solution
This is the fixer for cold-water dyes. Mix 200 gm (7 oz) of washing soda with hot water to make 1 litre (1¾ pints) of solution. Stir until dissolved and pour into the container.

23 *Left* A page from a dyeing file, with samples of fabrics and threads before and after dyeing. All information about quantities of dye powder, water, fabric and the length of time taken is carefully recorded with these samples

24 Very little equipment is needed for cold-water dyeing, and most items you will already have in the house. You do not need the small scales to begin with – dyes can be measured in measuring spoons. The rods are varnished so that they do not stain the dyebath

Hot-water dyeing method

1 Weigh 225 gm (8 oz) of fabric, or mixed fabric and threads. The fabric can be in one length or shorter pieces. Soak for one hour.

2 Put 3.45 litres (6 pints) of water in a jam pan.

3 Measure the dye. The quantity can be anything from ½ to 4 × 5 ml spoon (teaspoon) according to the strength of the colour required. For a first attempt use the whole of one small tin for this weight of fabric. Mix the dye with 1 tablespoon of cold water in a jam jar, and stir to make a paste. Add enough hot water to dissolve the powder (about one-third of the jar full). Stir well until the dye is properly dissolved – otherwise you will get blotches.

4 Add the dye to the jam pan, put it on the stove and heat.

5 Add the dripping wet fabric and stir. Bring to the boil, stirring frequently – about every five minutes.

6 Add 150 ml (5 fl oz) of salt solution in two stages while the dye is heating up, and another 75 ml (2½ fl oz) ten minutes after the dye has boiled. Remove the fabric while you add the solution. Boil for 20 or 30 minutes, or longer if you wish to get a deeper colour. Standardize the boiling time to enable you to repeat your results exactly. If you are dyeing silks with hot-water dyes, do not boil. Raise the temperature to 90°C (200°F) and keep it constant for 35-40 minutes.

7 Rinse the fabric until the water is clear, and then dry it.

25 Quilt with 37 different shades of blues and light oranges, made using strips sewn to a paper backing (method 3, page 40). Dyeing your own fabrics means that you can have a wider range of dyes than is commercially available. (*Valerie Campbell-Harding*)

Cold-water dyeing method

1 Weigh 225 gm (8 oz) of fabric or mixed fabrics and threads. Soak for one hour.

2 Put 3.45 litres (6 pints) of water in a plastic bucket.

3 Measure the dye. The quantity can be anything from ¼ to 4 × 5 ml spoon (teaspoon) according to the strength of colour required. A larger quantity does not make much difference and is expensive. For a first effort use the whole of one small tin. Mix the powder with 1 tablespoon of cold water in a jam jar and stir until it is a smooth paste. Add enough hot water (not boiling) to dissolve the dye, about one-third of the jar full.

4 Add the dye to the bucket and stir well.

5 Add the dripping wet fabric to the bucket and stir for five minutes. Leave for ten minutes for the dye to penetrate the fibres.

6 Remove the fabric from the bucket and add 300 ml (10 fl oz) for medium colours, or 450 ml (16 fl oz) for dark colours, of salt solution; stir and replace the fabric. Stir and agitate for 15 minutes. I do this by twisting and turning the fabric with my hands (in rubber gloves), and stirring with the stick. Every so often I lift up and open out the fabric to avoid the dye collecting in the creases. This is not necessary with threads.

7 Remove the fabric again. Add 225 ml (8 fl oz) of soda solution, stir and replace the fabric. Stir well and leave for at least one hour, and for up to four hours. Stir every five minutes for the first hour and every 15 minutes thereafter.

8 Remove the fabric from the bucket and pour away the dye, which is now exhausted.

9 Rinse until the water is clear. Then boil the fabric in water and a very little detergent for five minutes. Rinse and dry. If you are dyeing a fabric that should not be boiled, then add a little detergent to the fabric in a bucket, and pour over it a kettleful of boiling water. Leave for 15 minutes. Rinse and dry.

This method will give you a perfectly dyed length of fabric or skein of yarn with no blotches or streaks. If you wash the fabric, mix and dissolve the dye properly and stir enough, you will have no trouble.

26 Cushion made of cotton dyed in deep blue, cherry red and mixtures of these colours, to give three equal steps between the two pure colours. The centre of the cushion is of knitted torn strips, and the border is of log cabin patchwork. (*Valerie Campbell-Harding*)

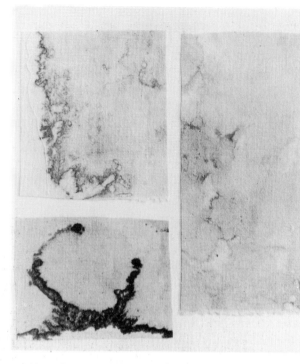

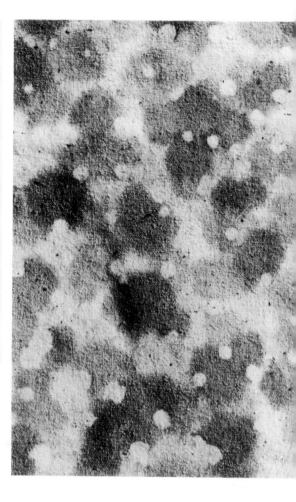

27 Dyes dropped with an eye dropper onto fabric painted with the solutions (left); and dyes mixed with salt and soda solutions dropped onto dry fabric (right)

28 *Right* Wax from a melting candle was dropped all over the fabric, then dark and pale blue dyes, mixed with salt and soda solution, were dropped on top

Experimental methods

There may be times when you do not want a smooth result and would like some texture or pattern on your fabric, or a multi-coloured effect. There are various experimental methods you can try out.

Dip-dyeing
You can use either the hot- or cold-water dyes for this. Simply dip part of a hank of threads, or part of the fabric, in the dye and leave for the required time. I would use a stronger solution than normal, to cut down on the time needed. When one area is dyed, remove the fabric or skein and dip another part of it in a dyebath of another colour. The

dye will spread and the colours will mix with each other. The fabric or skein must be boiled or cold-dyed for the proper length of time so that the colour is fixed, but you can have more than one piece going at the same time.

Spraying, painting, dabbing etc.
Cold-water dyes, mixed with some salt and soda solutions, can be sprayed onto fabric, painted or streaked onto it, or dabbed on with a sponge.
1 Mix about ½ × 5 ml spoon (teaspoon) of dye powder with 1 tablespoon of salt solution in a jar.
2 Add 1 tablespoon of soda solution and enough hot water to dissolve the dye.

3 Fill the jar up with cold water. This is a very strong mixture but you must still leave the solutions on the fabric long enough for them to work – at least 20 minutes.

An alternative is to mix 50 ml (2 fl oz) of salt solution and 75 ml (2½ fl oz) of soda solution in a jar with cold water to fill it, and paint this onto the fabric until it is saturated, then apply the dye – either in liquid or powder form. If using the powder, I put a little in a square of muslin, tie it up into a bag, then *gently* shake it onto the fabric to make coloured spots. Again leave it to fix.

Space dyeing

This is a different method of producing a multi-coloured fabric. You can use any two or three colours, but those that contrast strongly are the best, otherwise they blend too well and are uninteresting.

First method

1 Tear 10 cm (4 in.) wide strips of fabric 46 cm (18 in.) long and tie a long skein of thread at intervals. Place the fabric and thread around the edge of a baking dish or cat litter tray. The skein should go all the way round. Soak for one hour or use dry.
2 Mix ½ × 5 ml spoon (teaspoon) of cold-water dye powder in a jam jar with 1 tablespoon of salt solution.
3 Add enough hot water to dissolve the dye, and fill the jar up with cold water. Do the same with the other colours, each one in a separate jar.
4 Spoon the dyes onto the fabric strips at intervals. Do not mix the colours too much, or they will loose their identity. Leave for five minutes for the dye to penetrate.
5 Mix 100 ml (3½ fl oz) of soda solution with about 850 ml (1½ pints) of water. Pour this over the fabrics, making sure that everything is covered. Leave for half an hour.
6 Pour the dye away, rinse and wash as usual. Do not be horrified at the murky liquid in the dish — the fabric will be beautiful at the end of the process.

Second method

1 Mix the dye with the salt solution as before in a slightly larger jar.
2 Add 2 tablespoons of soda solution to each jar, dissolve the dye in hot water, and fill up with cold water.
3 Spoon this mixture over the fabrics at intervals and leave for half an hour.
4 Pour the dye away, rinse and wash

This method gives more distinct areas of colour with less mixing than the first method.

Using all three primary colours gives a lovely mixture of subtle as well as bright colours, and using any two complementary colours works well. Close, or analogous, colours are too similar and the result is not very exciting. Strongly contrasting tones are worth trying, for example navy blue and pale green, or light and dark of the same colour.

29 Samples of space-dyed fabrics. Silk organza, silk habutai, silk noil, silk crêpe and unbleached calico were all dyed together to give a range of tones. The dye affects the various fabrics differently

30 Cushion using space-dyed silk, cotton and velvet. The applied flower is pin-tucked for added texture, and the border is strip patchwork using strips sewn to a fabric backing (method 4, page 42) (*Helen Robertson*)

31 Corner of a cushion in which some of the fabrics have been tea-dyed to soften the colours

Dyeing with tea

This is a useful method to tone down a colour that is too bright, or to soften a print that is too contrasty. Garish yellows become soft golds, bright reds turn into turkey reds, and electric blues into greyed turquoises. Tea dyeing gives an antique look to new fabrics, and this is useful in conservation work.

Black tea gives the best results, and the permanence is fairly good, especially if vinegar is used. This method is not exact as tea varies so much, but once you have done one batch, you can repeat it exactly or vary it as you wish. No mordant is needed for this dye, as the tannic acid in the tea sets in the dye.

1 Wash and rinse the fabrics as usual. Soak for one hour if dry.
2 Put 10-20 tea bags in a jam pan.
3 Add 11.5 litres (20 pints) of cold water, bring to the boil, and boil for ten minutes. Remove the tea bags.
4 Add the fabric – up to 700 g (1½ lb) for this quantity of dye, if your pan is big enough.
5 Boil for 15 minutes, stirring frequently to avoid blotches.
6 Add 275 ml (½ pint) of white vinegar.
7 Boil for a further ten minutes, stirring frequently.
8 Rinse, wash if necessary, and rinse again.

These instructions are for cotton fabrics. If you are using silks keep the temperature at 90°C (200°F). Do not allow to boil.

Dyeing with onion skins

This is another natural dye that does not need a mordant and is very fast. It usually gives a lovely golden colour, and can be used to over-dye coloured or patterned fabrics, or on cream or white ones. Save your onion skins until you have a bagful and weigh them for future reference.

1 Place the onion skins in a jam pan and cover with cold water.

2 Boil for one hour to extract the colour, adding more water if necessary. You can use this liquor, or freeze it for the future. Throw away the skins.

3 Measure the liquor. You will need 3. 45 litres (6 pints) to dye 225 gm (8 oz) of fabric. Return to the pan.

4 Soak the fabric for one hour.

5 Add the wet fabric to the pan.

6 Simmer for 30 minutes or more, stirring frequently.

7 Rinse, wash and rinse again to remove the smell.

32 Cushion combining a mixture of fabrics dyed soft creamy-yellow in onion skins. (*Valerie Campbell-Harding*)

33 Cushion combining space-dyed fabrics, sprayed fabrics and plain colours dyed to match. The flower is applied, with added machine and hand embroidery. The strips were added log cabin fashion (method 7, page 48). (*Valerie Campbell-Harding*)

Bleaching or discharge dyeing

Using household bleach to give a range of tones and colours from one fabric is often not considered. You can bleach plain or patterned fabrics, and it is amazing how many colours and tones you can get from a single fabric. I use bleach only on cotton as it rots silk, and does not usually work on man-made fibres.

1 Wash and rinse all fabrics as before.
2 Mix 1 part bleach to 20 parts water. Make enough to cover the fabric well.
3 Add the fabric and leave for five minutes to 24 hours, depending on the fastness of the dye. Stir frequently to avoid blotches. However, if you wish to have a textured fabric, crumple the fabric up and leave it without stirring.
4 Rinse the bleach out.
5 To kill the bleach and prevent the fabric rotting, mix 1 x 5 ml spoon (teaspoon) sodium metabisulphate in a bucket of cold water, add the fabric and leave it for five minutes. Rinse well. This also takes away any smell from your hands.

Experimental bleaching
A stronger solution of bleach can be used for spraying, tie-bleaching (the opposite of tie-dyeing), or for dropping or painting streaks or blobs onto fabric. Mix 1 part bleach with 2-4 parts water. Use sodium metabisulphate to neutralize as before.

You will find that some dyes will not be affected at all, and some will bleach very fast indeed.There is also a difference between the colours. It is worth making detailed notes, and keeping samples of the original fabrics as well as the bleached ones.

34 Bleached fabrics.The original fabric is on the left. The central sample was bleached for 20 minutes, and the right-hand sample for one hour. These times are not a guide, as fabrics vary a great deal

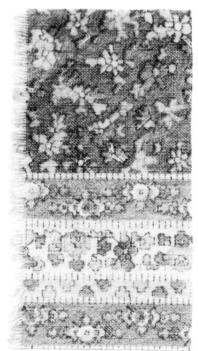

Sewing Methods

There are several ways of sewing strips of fabric together, depending on the effect that you want, and whether the work is to be quilted or not. I have grouped them all together in one section for convenience, as many of the designs in this book can be sewn by more than one method.

For most methods, the fabric should be carefully marked with a permanent pen or a hard pencil, and cut with sharp scissors. Use a metre or yard stick and draw the lines across the width of the fabric. Measure the widths of the strips with a ruler, or use plastic or card strips cut to the correct width as a guide.

For one or two methods you can tear the strips, but this tends to distort the edges and makes accurate sewing difficult. It is not a good idea to cut strips longer than 1.5 metres (yards) as they become unwieldy. I suggest that you clear a large enough space on a table and work with the fabric spread out flat. The drawing and

cutting of the lines must be absolutely accurate or you will have trouble later when sewing the strips together.

Use large scissors for cutting out, with long blades. Again, this makes for accuracy. Some people are very successful with roller cutters, but I am not. Also, I find that the fabric tends to slip if I cut through more than one layer at a time. Cutting the strips is the tedious part of the process, but it is worth having one good session and getting all the strips cut out at one go, rather than to keep stopping to cut just one more when you are in the middle of sewing. Hang the strips on the back of a chair or over a clothes dryer, in their colour families so that it is easy to pick out what you want. You are now ready to start sewing.

The following methods are all numbered, and the captions to the illustrations in the rest of the book give the number of the method used, where relevant.

Each method has its advantages and disadvantages, and the one you choose depends very much on the use to which the patchwork will be put. If you wish to quilt your work, then do not choose a method that is sewn to a backing or one that is folded, as there will be too much bulk. I am sure that there are still other methods, and do not pretend that I have listed them all. However, these should cover your needs.

The strips can be any width from 6 mm (1/4 in.) (finished width) upwards. You need 6 mm (1/4 in.) seam allowance on each side, and so the narrowest strip you are likely to want will be 18 mm (3/4 in.). If the strip is narrower than this there will be too much bulk at the seam unless the fabric is very fine. If you wish to have strips narrower than 6 mm (1/4 in.) I suggest you use method 4 (strips sewn to a backing fabric) as it is possible to get strips as narrow as 1.5 mm (1/16 in.) by this method.

Method 1 — Machine-pieced straight strips

1 Mark your strips on the fabric, using a permanent fine pen, or a hard pencil. They should be the finished width plus 13 mm (½ in.) seam allowance (6 mm [¼ in.] each side). Cut out carefully.

2 Pin two strips together, right sides facing each other, with the raw edges matching. The pins should go at right angles to the edges *(35a)*.

3 Stitch, keeping the edge of the presser foot on the edge of the fabrics *(35b)*. You can sew over the pins, or take them out as you come to them. If you find puckering occurs, then check your stitch and bobbin tensions. When sewing very narrow strips, say 6 mm (¼ in.) finished width, stitch the first seam, then use this line of stitching as a guide for sewing the second seam, keeping the edge of the presser foot on the first line of stitches *(35c)*.

4 Press the seams open, or to one side, depending on where your quilting stitches (if any) are to go.

NB When seaming long strips together, sew each seam from the opposite end to avoid the work curving *(35d)*. This does not happen so much with short strips.

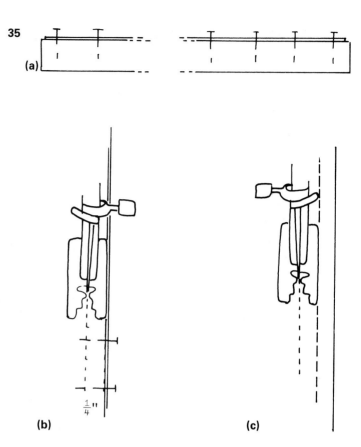

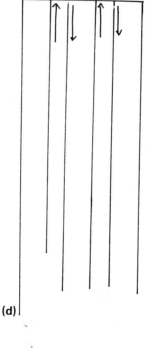

36 *Opposite* Strips of silk, cottons and rayons sewn together by the pieced strips method (method 1, page 36). As the strips are of uneven widths it is not necessary to match the seams

37 A cushion with pieced strips of different widths, and added embroidery. (*Andrea Statham*)

38 A simple cushion using both sides of a furnishing fabric. (*Valerie Campbell-Harding*)

39 A bag using strips of flowered cotton fabrics, quilted to give body. (*Valerie Campbell-Harding*)

36

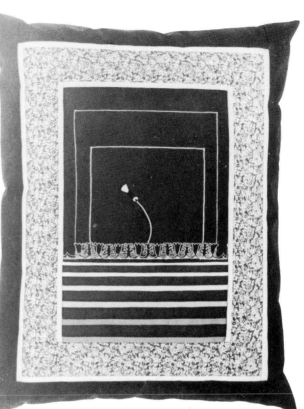

37

38

39

Method 2 — Machine-pieced curved strips

1   Make the templates. Draw the design on paper, very accurately.
2   Mark the balance marks across all seams *(40a)*. Short seams might need only one mark, but longer seams need five or six. These marks are essential for the accurate matching of seams when sewing.
3   Carefully cut out the shapes. Glue them to thin card, leaving enough space between each shape for the addition of seam allowances.
4   Measure and draw 6 mm (¼ in.) seam allowances on all sides of each template *(40b)*.
5   Carefully cut out the templates *(40c)*, using a knife if possible. Do not try to cut right through the card in one go, but cut gently two or three times, going slowly around the curves.
6   Place the templates *upside-down* on the *wrong* side of the fabric, matching any straight edges to the grain of the fabric if possible. Draw around the edge of the template with a hard pencil, making sure that the sharp point of the pencil touches the edge of the card. Mark the balance marks on the fabric.
7   Cut the fabric out as carefully as you can, using very sharp scissors.
8   Hold two fabric pieces together, right sides facing, matching the balance marks at the centre of the seam *(40d)*. Pin at right angles to the seam. Pin the two edges together *(40e)* and then the other balance marks. Extra pins may be added if needed *(40f)*.
9   Stitch 6 mm (¼ in.) away from the raw edges, keeping the edge of the presser foot on the edge of the fabric.
10   press the seam open, or as it falls naturally – which is usually towards the concave side of the seam.

Hand-piecing curved strips
If you wish to sew curved strips by hand, make your templates *without* any seam allowance. Draw around the template on to the fabric, then cut the shape out adding 6 mm (¼ in.) seam allowance. You can judge this by eye. Then pin as before. Stitch with a tiny running stitch on the drawn line.

40

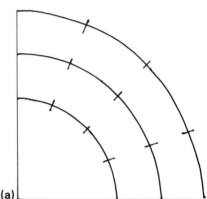

(a)

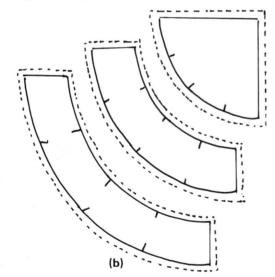

(b)

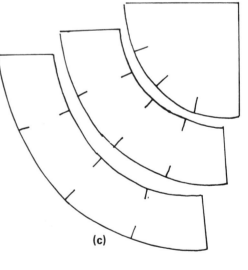

(c)

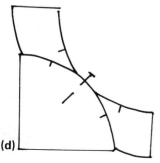

(d)

(e)

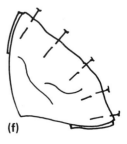

(f)

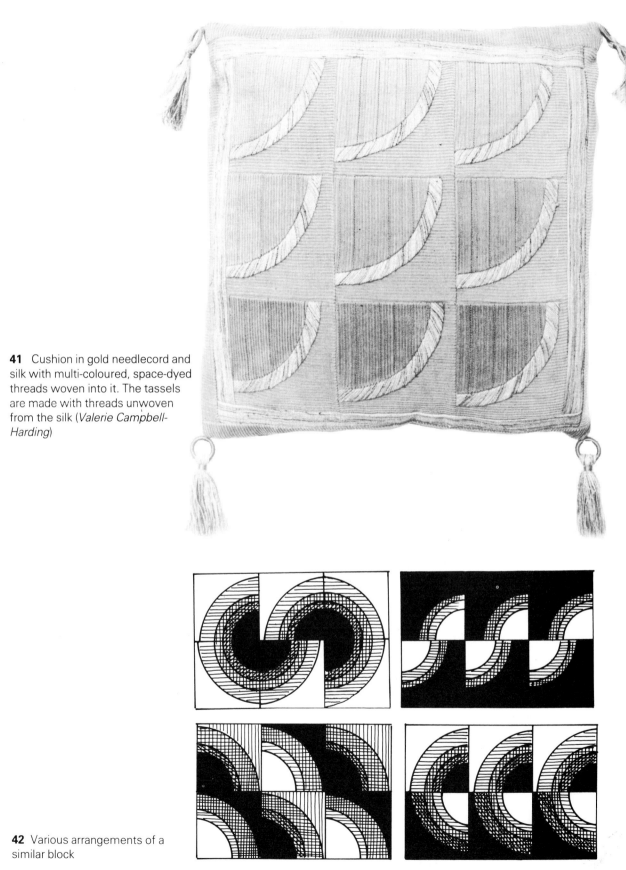

41 Cushion in gold needlecord and silk with multi-coloured, space-dyed threads woven into it. The tassels are made with threads unwoven from the silk (*Valerie Campbell-Harding*)

42 Various arrangements of a similar block

Method 3 — Strips sewn to a paper backing

43

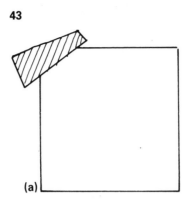

(a)

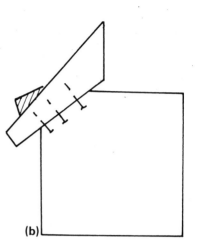

(b)

1   Draw a square on greaseproof paper. A good size of square for a quilt is 15–20 cm (6-8 in.), but if smaller squares are wanted, draw a 25 cm (10 in.) square and cut it into four when you have sewn it.

2   Cut strips or wedges at random from fabrics.

3   Starting in one corner of the drawn square, lay a short strip of fabric across the corner, with the fabric right side up *(43a)*.

4   Lay another strip on top, wrong side up, matching the edges. Pin through both layers of fabric and through the paper, with the pins at right angles to the fabric edges *(43b)*.

5   Stitch through all the layers with a 6 mm (¼ in.) seam allowance, using the edge of the presser foot as a guide.

6   Fold the top strip forward and press *(43c)*.

7   Lay the third strip on top, wrong side up, matching edges. Pin *(43d)*, stitch and press as before.

8   Continue until the whole square is covered, using longer strips across the centre of the square *(43e)*.

9   Turn the square over and cut through all the layers on the drawn lines.

10   Gently pull the paper away, leaving an accurate fabric square *(43f)*.

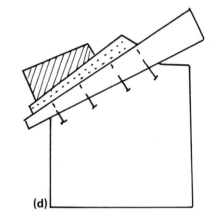

(c)

(d)

When a number of squares have been made, they can be sewn together in a variety of patterns. It is advisable to stitch the squares together through another strip of paper to avoid any stretching of the bias edges.

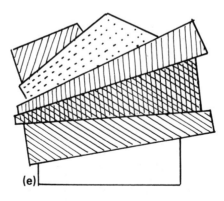

(e)

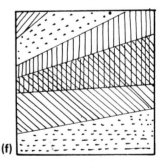

(f)

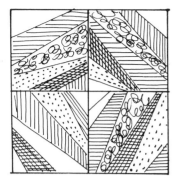

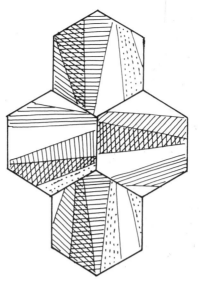

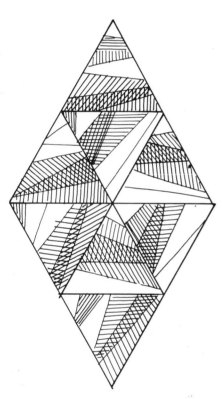

44 Various shapes and patterns using method 3. Wedges, rather than straight strips, give much more movement to the designs

45 *Below* Detail of a quilt. (*Elizabeth Heitzmann*)

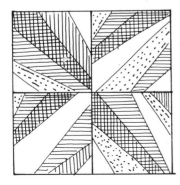

Method 4 — Strips sewn to a fabric backing

This method gives really accurate strips, as wide or as narrow as you like.

1 Draw a square, rectangle or the shape of the article that you wish to make on calico or other backing fabric. The shape must be slightly larger than required.

2 Carefully measure, draw and cut strips of fabric of the required finished width plus 12 mm (½ in.) seam allowance. (I never cut strips less than 25 mm [1 in.] wide, even if they are to be only 3 mm [⅛ in.] when finished, as narrow strips are difficult to handle.) The strips must be long enough to cover the drawn lines.

3 Draw guide lines on the backing fabric (46a). These do not need to be the same as the finished pattern, but they must be parallel to each other and at right angles to the sides. I use the width of the ruler.

4 Place the first strip face up on the backing with one edge against the line x-x. Place the second strip face down on top of it, matching the edges. Pin through all layers at right angles to the edges. Stitch through all the layers 6 mm (¼ in.) from the edges of the strips, using the presser foot as a guide (46b). Fold the second strip forward and press. Measure and draw a line on the top of the second fabric which is the required finished width of that strip plus 6 mm (¼ in.) seam allowance, y-y (46c).

5 Place the third strip face down on top of the second strip with one long edge touching the drawn line. Measure back from one of the guide lines to check that it is straight. Pin, * stitch (46d) and press as before.

6 Continue until the whole of the shape is covered.

46

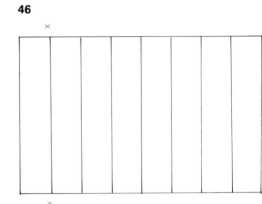

(a)

Narrow strips
The above method works for strips that are fairly wide, but if you wish to have narrow strips (6 mm [¼ in.] or less), then some of the seams must be stitched from the wrong side for greater accuracy.

Follow the instructions until *. Then turn the work over, measure and draw your next stitching line on the backing fabric. Stitch on the drawn line. Then turn the work over to the front again and continue as above.

An alternative to drawing the stitching line is to use the presser foot as a guide, with one edge touching the previous stitching line.

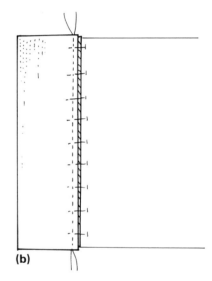

(b)

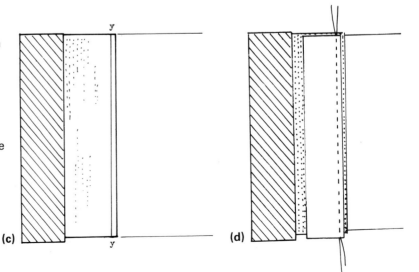

(c)   **(d)**

47 Silk ties (*Andrea Statham*)

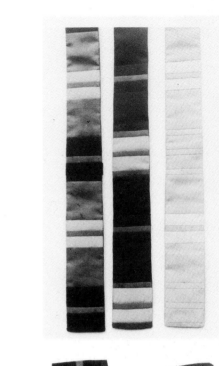

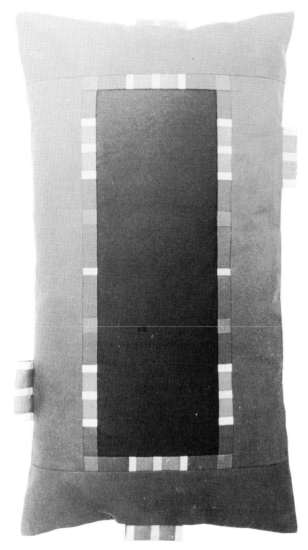

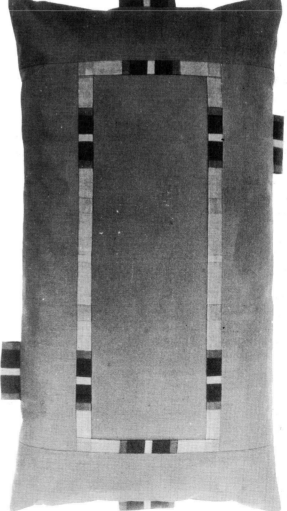

48 Tabbed cushions. The large plain areas focus attention on the stripes. (*Andrea Statham*)

Method 5 — Bias-backed strips

This method gives a completely bias result and is useful for ties and some garments. The paper backing supports the calico backing which is on the bias and might otherwise stretch while being stitched.

1 Make a thin card template, the shape of the article you wish to make, including 6 mm (¼ in.) seam allowance around all the edges.

2 Place this template on fine calico or other backing fabric, on the bias. (In the diagrams the arrow marks the straight grain.) Draw round the template with a hard pencil or permanent pen. Cut out the calico, leaving at least 12 mm (½ in.) all round the edge.

3 Pin the backing shape to greaseproof paper.

4 Draw guide lines on the straight grain of the fabric, inside the drawn shape *(49a)*. These do not need to be the same as the finished pattern, but they must be parallel to each other.

5 Carefully measure, draw and cut strips of fabric (on the straight grain), the required finished width plus 12 mm (½ in.) seam allowance. The strips must be long enough to cover the drawn lines.

6 Place the first strip face down on the backing, covering the first edge of the drawn shape. Place the second strip face down on top of it, matching the edges. Pin through all layers of fabric and paper, with the pins at right angles to the edge *(49b)*. Stitch through all the layers 6 mm (¼ in.) from the edge of the

strips, using the presser foot as a guide. Fold the second strip forward and press.

7 Measure and draw a line on the second strip of the required finished width of the strip plus 6 mm (¼ in.) seam allowance. Check that it is straight by measuring from a guide line.

8 Place the third strip face down touching the drawn line. Pin, stitch and press as before. If the strip is to be narrower than 12 mm (½ in.), it is a good idea to stitch from the back as in method 4.

9 Continue until the whole of the backing is covered. Then place the card template on top of the patchwork and draw round the edge. Cut it out. Gently tear the paper away from the back. Make up the article.

49

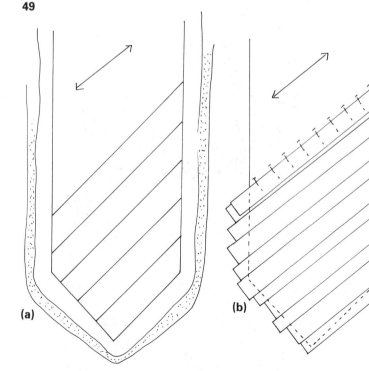

(a)   (b)

50 *Opposite* A variation of method 5. (a) Draw a rectangle on a backing fabric twice as long as it is wide. Draw lines from the centre of the sides to the opposite corners
(b) Mark equal sections on both sides of the rectangle and join up the marks
(c) Sew strips to the backing as in the instructions
(d) Trim off surplus ends and corner triangles
(e) Mark and cut patchwork into vertical strips
(f) Reverse alternate strips and seam together
(g), (h) Completed long diamond shapes can be sewn to other strips and plain pieces to make border patterns

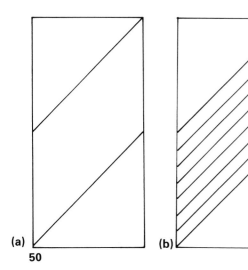

(a)
50

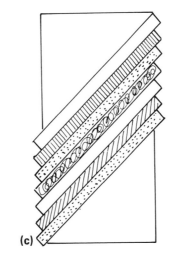

(b)

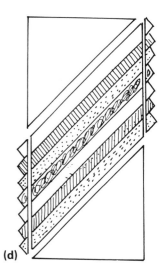

(c)

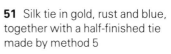

(d)

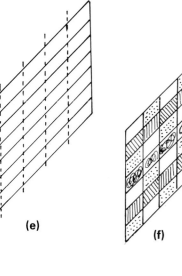

(e)

(f)

51 Silk tie in gold, rust and blue, together with a half-finished tie made by method 5

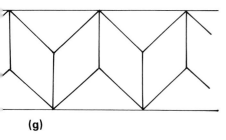

(g)

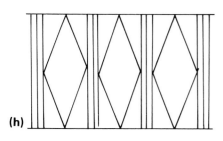

(h)

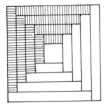

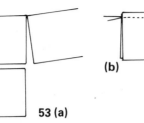

(b)

53 (a)

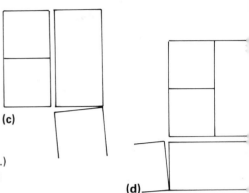

(c)

(d)

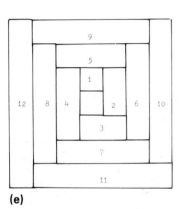

(e)

Method 6 — Pieced log cabin

Log cabin patchwork is the most common name given to the pattern in which strips are sewn to a central square, working outwards from the centre to the edges of the block. This method is the one to use when you wish to quilt your patchwork, as there is little bulk.

There are two sewing sequences: in one the strips are sewn in a spiral, in the other they are sewn in opposite pairs.

Spiral method (52)
1 Draw and cut 38 mm (1½ in.) wide strips of fabric, some light and some dark. Draw and cut a 38 mm (1½ in.) square for the centre.
2 Place one light strip next to one edge of the square and cut it to match. Place it face down on top of the square and pin along one edge *(53a)*.
3 Stitch 6 mm (¼ in.) from the edge using running stitch if sewing by hand, or a machine straight stitch *(53b)*.
4 Fold the strip back and press, leaving the raw edges facing outwards from the square. Hold the second light strip against the edge of the square plus the width of the first strip, and cut it to fit. Stitch and press as before *(53c)*.
5 Measure and cut a third strip, this time dark. Pin, stitch and press *(53d)*.
6 Measure and cut a fourth strip, also dark. Pin, stitch and press.
7 Continue in this way, sewing two light and two dark strips in every round until the block is large enough *(53e)*.

Opposite pairs method (54)
(sometimes called courthouse steps)
1 Cut the strips and central square as before.
2 Place one light strip on one edge of the square; pin, stitch and press *(55a)*. Place another light strip on the opposite side, pin, stitch and press.
3 Place two dark strips on the other two sides, pin, stitch and press *(55b)*.
4 Continue sewing the strips in pairs, keeping the lights and darks opposite each other, until the block is large enough *(55c)*.

Of course you can vary the placing of the light and dark strips in either method, but these are the basic instructions.

When enough blocks are finished sew them together using a 6 mm (¼ in.) seam.

54 Opposite pairs method

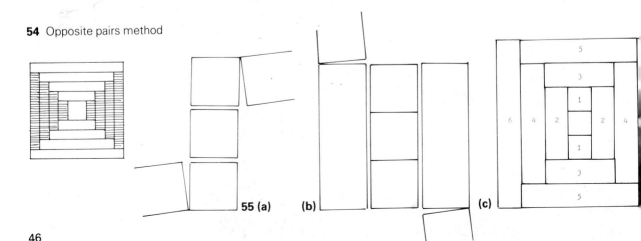

55 (a) **(b)** **(c)**

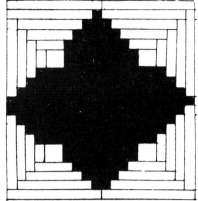

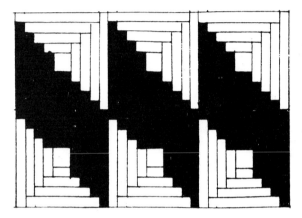
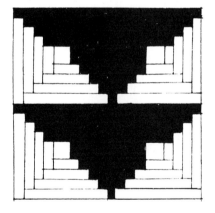
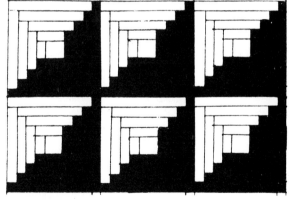

56 Design suggestions for pieced log cabin

Method 7 — Log cabin on a fabric backing

1 Draw a square (about 20-25 cm/8-10 in.) on a piece of calico or other backing fabric. Draw diagonals from corner to corner to find the centre. Draw two more guide lines on each side of the square, parallel to the outer edge *(57a)*.

2 Cut a 38 mm (1½ in.) square of coloured fabric. Place it on the centre of the calico square matching the corners to the diagonal lines. Pin in place *(57b)*.

3 Measure, mark and carefully cut 25-38 mm (1-1½ in.) strips of coloured fabric.

4 You can use either the spiral or the opposite pairs sewing sequence for this block, but these instructions will be for the opposite sequence. Place one light strip next to one edge of the square and cut it to match. Cut another one the same *(51c)*. Place one of the strips on top of the square, face down, matching edges. Pin. Stitch 6 mm (¼ in.) away from the edge through all the layers. Fold the strip forward and press. Stitch the second light strip on the opposite side of the square. Fold forward and press.

5 Place two dark strips on the other two sides. Cut, pin, stitch and press as before *(57d)*.

6 Continue sewing the strips in pairs until the square is full, checking by the guide lines that each one is in the right place, and parallel to the outer edge of the square *(57e, f)*.

If you wish to sew very narrow strips, I suggest that you draw the stitching line on the back, and stitch on that line, parallel to the previous stitching line. (See method 4).

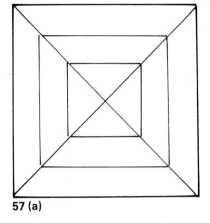

57 (a)

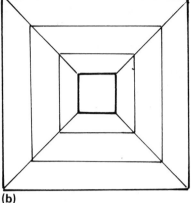

(b)

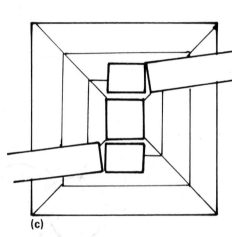

(c)

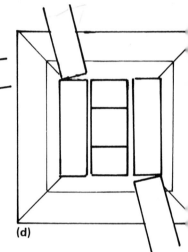

(d)

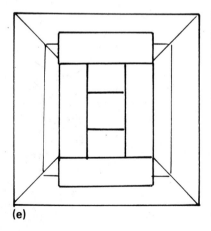

(e)

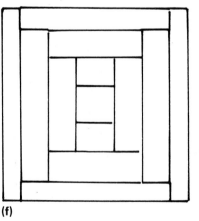

(f)

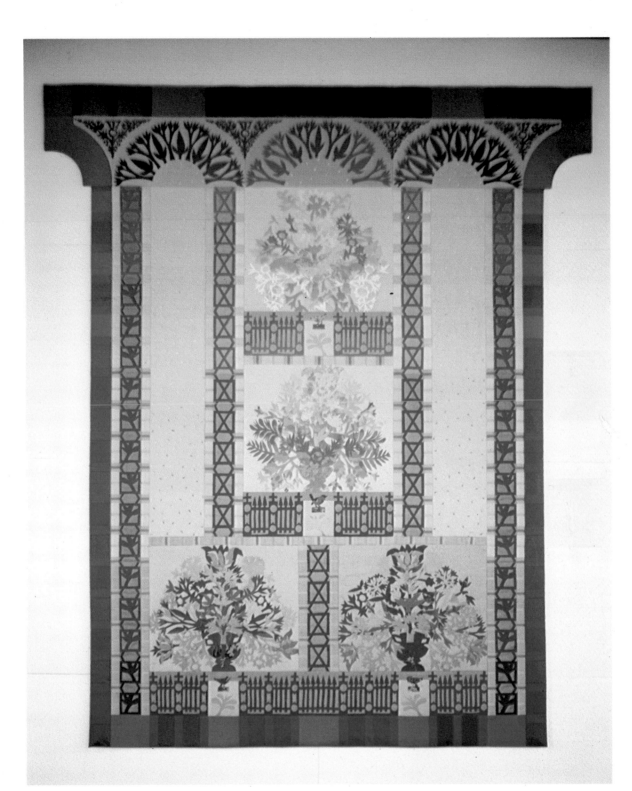

1 Wall hanging of pieced, quilted and embroidered silk fabrics (180 cm x 136 cm — 6 ft x 4 ft 6 in.). The flowers are applied and embroidered, and the borders are all pieced onto a fabric backing. (*Andrea Statham*)

2 Hanging cushion using hand-dyed silks and cottons. The strips are sewn to a backing (method 4) with folded triangles inserted in the seams. The chenille cords support the small cushions. (*Valerie Campbell-Harding*)

3 Cushion of hand-dyed cottons. The textured areas are plaited strips of fabric, space-dyed. The cushion was constructed by method 4 (sewn to a fabric backing) with folded squares inserted into the seams. (*Valerie Campbell-Harding*)

58 Cushion made using method 7. The shot silk gives tonal variation because of the change of direction of the strips. (*Valerie Campbell-Harding*)

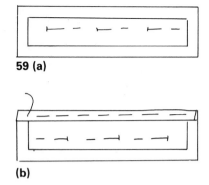

59 (a)

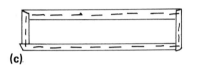

(b)

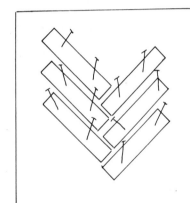

(c)

(d)

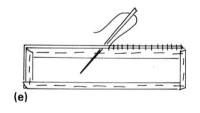

(e)

Method 8 — Paper-backed strips

In this method the fabric is tacked over paper or card templates and the patches are oversewn together by hand. It is an extremely accurate method, although time-consuming. With some patterns, it is the only method that can be used.

1 Measure and draw your strips onto stiff paper, or graph paper. Cut them out carefully, with a knife rather than scissors.
2 Pin the paper strip to the wrong side of the fabric, and cut the fabric out round the paper, leaving about 6 mm (¼ in.) seam allowance on all edges *(59a)*.
3 Turn the fabric over the paper and tack through all the layers, leaving the ends of the thread hanging so that it is easy to remove when you have finished the sewing *(59b, c)*
4 Stab-pin the tacked shapes to a piece of polystyrene or a cork bath mat in the pattern that you have designed. This is important so that you sew the correct edges to each other *(59d)*.
5 Remove two adjacent strips, place them face to face, and oversew them together with tiny stitches. Do not go through the paper. Start the sewing with a back stitch and finish with another one. Knots will make bumps on the right side of the patchwork if the fabric is fine *(59e)*.
6 When two pieces have been sewn together, replace them on the board. Take two more and sew them.
7 When the sewing is finished, press the work on the back, remove the tacking threads and papers, and lightly press again.

When you are sewing curved edges together, you will have to bend the shapes so that only a small section of the edges fit together. It looks strange while you are doing it, but correct when they are laid flat again.

60 A chevron pattern as a skirt border. Slubbed silks ranging from white through yellow, orange and reds to black

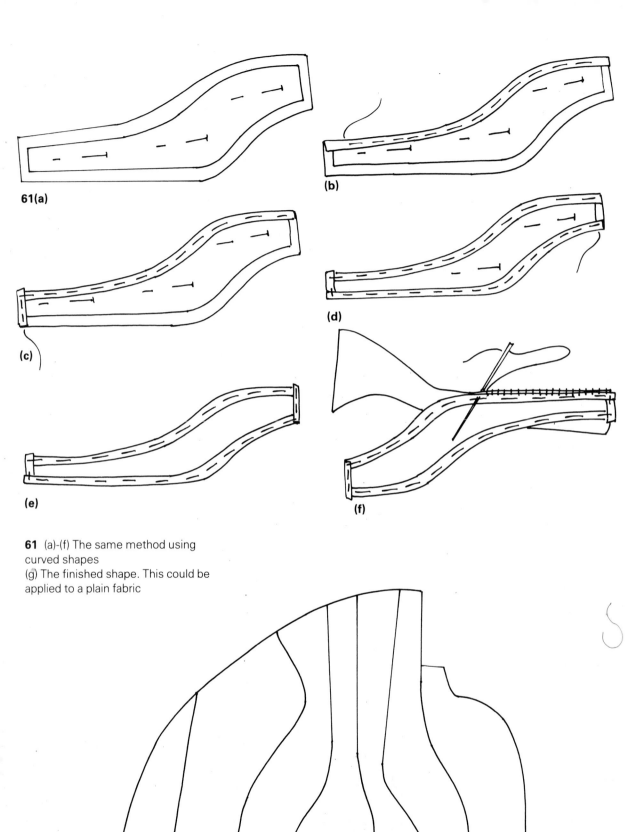

61(a)

(b)

(c)

(d)

(e)

(f)

61 (a)-(f) The same method using curved shapes
(g) The finished shape. This could be applied to a plain fabric

(g)

Method 9 — Wadded strips

This method sews the patchwork and quilts it at the same time.

1 Place a piece of calico or other backing fabric, slightly larger than you need, flat on a table. Lay a sheet of wadding of about the same size on top.

2 Pin at the corners, then around the edge, then in central area. Put in enough pins to hold the two layers securely.

3 Tack around the edge. Next tack in vertical and horizontal lines, making a grid. The lines should not be more than 20-25 cm (8-10 in.) apart, and I prefer them to be even closer than this *(62a)*.

4 Mark guide lines on the wadding with a felt-tip pen. These do not have to be the same as the final pattern, but they should be parallel *(62b)*.

5 Lay the first strip face up with one edge touching the first guide line.

6 Lay the second strip face down with the edges matching.

7 Pin through all the layers, with the pins at right angles to the edge. Seam a good 6 mm (¼ in.) away from the edge. Fold the strip forwards, but do not press it or you will melt the wadding *(62c)*.

8 Lay the third strip face down on top, check that it is straight by measuring from the next guide line, pin and stitch *(62d)*.

9 Continue until the whole backing is covered. Trim the edges.

I have used this method on the diagonal for a cushion cover and it works perfectly well except that it distorts the backing, because you are continually sewing on the bias. The solution is to make the whole thing larger than you need, and then cut it to the correct shape afterwards.

62

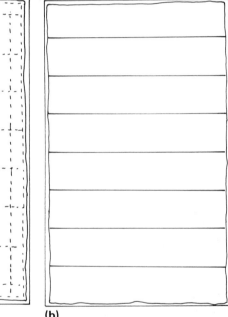

(a)

(b)

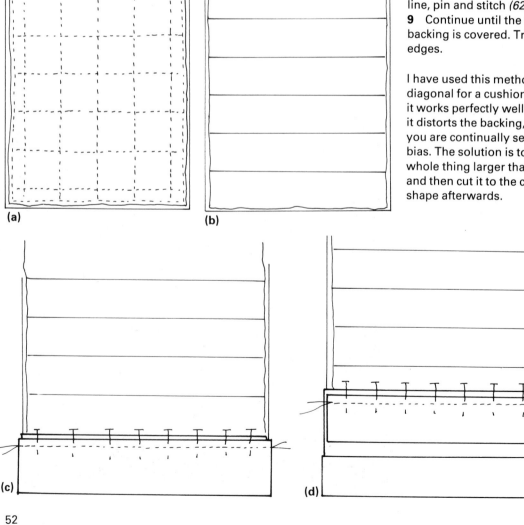

(c)

(d)

64 Handkerchief case in red printed cotton fabrics

65 Cushion in pinks, wines and black, using mixed fabrics. (*Anne Ohlenschlager*)

63 Christmas stocking in red and green cotton fabrics

Method 10 — Folded log cabin

These instructions are for the opposite sequence of sewing the strips, but folded log cabin could equally well be made using the spiral sequence.

1 Tear (or cut) strips of coloured fabric 5-10 cm (2-4 in.) wide. Fold in half lengthways and press.
2 Cut a 38 mm (1½ in.) square of coloured fabric.
3 Draw a square of 20-25 cm (8-10 in.) on a piece of calico or other backing fabric. Draw diagonals from corner to corner *(66a)*.
4 Place the coloured square in the centre of the calico square, matching the corners to the diagonal lines. Pin in place *(66b)*.
5 Place one folded strip next to one edge of the square and cut it to match. Cut another one the same.
6 Place one strip on top of the coloured square, with raw edges matching. Pin at right angles to the edge. Stitch by hand or machine through all the layers. This can be a straight stitch, or zigzag if the fabric frays readily. Stitch the second strip to the opposite side of the square in the same way *(66c)*. (Do not fold these strips back as in the other log cabin methods.)
7 Measure and cut two strips for the other two sides of the square, pin and stitch as before *(66d)*.
8 Continue building the pattern out to the edges, each round overlapping the previous round to hide the stitches. Continually measure in from the outside drawn edge to check that the strips are parallel to it *(66e, f)*.

Overlapping strips can also make a straight or diagonal pattern, but they must not be too long or they will bend back to show the stitching. Decorative stitching could be added to secure these layers. Narrow bands of folded strips can be inserted between two seams.

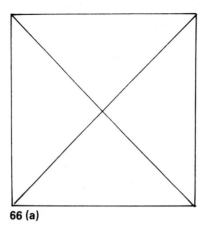

66 (a)

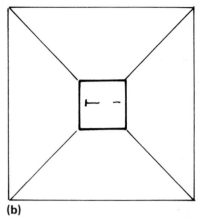

(b)

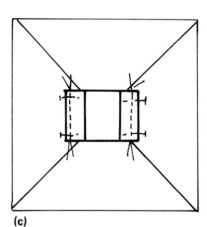

(c)

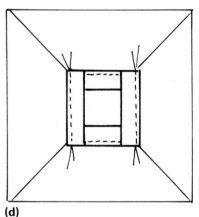

(d)

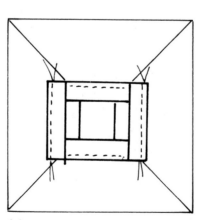

(e)

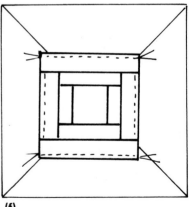

(f)

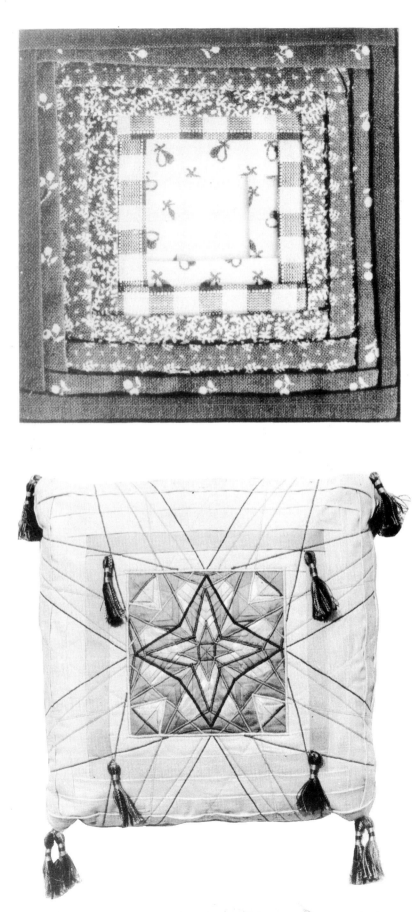

67 Log cabin using folded strips. The colours range from black to white, giving an impression of recession

68 Folded log cabin using shot silk. Quilting wool was threaded through each pleat as it was sewn on

69 *Left* Cushion with folded strips making a border to a central square of folded triangles. Organza was laid over the top of the centre square, some satin stitch bars were added, and parts of the organza were cut away. The folded strips were added next, with more stitching to secure them

55

Method 11 — Pleated strips on a fabric backing

1 Cut a piece of calico, or other backing fabric, a little larger than the required finished size. This can be a square or rectangle, or it can be part of a garment.

2 Draw lines 12 mm (½ in.) apart on the calico.

3 Cut or tear 50 cm (2 in.) strips of fabric.

4 Lay the first strip with one edge touching the first drawn line, face up.

5 Lay the second strip face down on top of it, matching the raw edges.

6 Stitch 6 mm (¼ in.) away from the edges using the presser foot as a guide.

7 Fold the top strip over to touch the second drawn line, and press it.

8 Lay the third strip face down on top of the second strip, matching the raw edges. Stitch, fold and press as before.

9 Continue until the backing is covered. Trim the edges to the required shape.

70 A sample of pleated strips in progress

Method 12 — Frayed strips

It is possible simply to sew strips of fabric together with the seam on the right side and fray them afterwards, but the result is a little thin looking. This method is better.

1 Tear (not cut) 5 cm (2 in.) strips of fabric and hang them over the back of a chair in colour families.

2 Take six strips of fabric in different colours and carefully lay them on top of one another on a table. The edges must all match. The top and bottom strips are the ones that will show on the right side of the patchwork, so the bottom strip must be face down on the table, and the top strip face up.

3 Pin all along one edge, with the pins at right angles to the fabric.

4 Stitch 6 mm (¼ in.) away from the edges, over the pins. Remove the pins and press the seam open from the back. Fray all the edges on the narrow side of the stitching half way back to the seam. You will now have six colours showing at the seam.

5 Repeat this with six more strips. Make up as many of these pairs as you need, and then join the pairs together, with the seam on the right side of the work.

71 Detail of the jacket shown in colour plate 6 made by method 12

Method 13 — Vilene-backed strips

1 Cut a piece of soft iron-on vilene slightly larger than the finished required size. It can be any shape.

2 Draw the pattern accurately onto the *shiny* side of the vilene.

3 Measure, draw and carefully cut strips of fabric the exact width and length for the pattern.

4 Place the piece of vilene flat on a table or ironing-board. Starting at one edge, place your strips in position, leaving no gaps between them.

5 When several strips are in place, iron them carefully, making sure that the iron does not touch the vilene. Place a few more strips in position, and iron them. Continue until the pattern is complete.

6 Turn the work over and iron from the back. Allow to cool.

7 Thread up your sewing machine with a colour that tones with all the fabrics in the patchwork. Sew zigzag (or satin) stitch over all the raw edges, with the stitch extending equally on either side of the join *(72a, b)*.

When you wish to travel from one place to another and the join has already been sewn, change the stitch to a normal straight stitch; sew this on top of the zigzag until you reach the point where you wish to start the zigzag again. The straight stitches will hardly show at all.

This method works equally well for straight or curved strips, which can be quilted. The patchwork can be washed, which helps to make it softer.

72

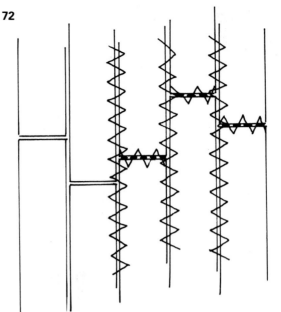

(a)

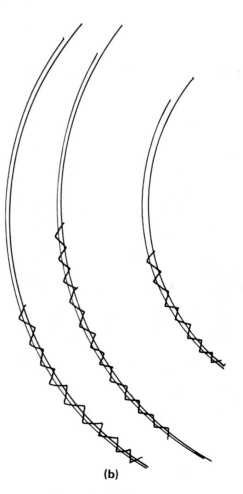

(b)

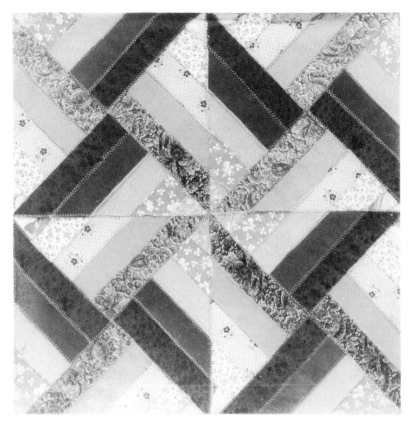

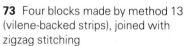

73 Four blocks made by method 13 (vilene-backed strips), joined with zigzag stitching

74 A table mat using the same method, in browns and blacks. It is backed with towelling and the edges are bound with a bias strip. (*Valerie Campbell-Harding*)

Method 14 — Bonded strips

This method uses *Bondaweb*, a paper-backed web of glue, which is ironed onto the back of fabrics. These fabrics can then be bonded onto another fabric. The advantage this method has over Method 13 is that small or large areas can be bonded onto another fabric, leaving spaces in between. The disadvantage is that it is more difficult to work.

1   Cut pieces of the fabrics you wish to use. These can be any size up to 46 × 46 cm (18 × 18 in.). Cut a piece (or pieces) of *Bondaweb* to fit the fabric pieces. Check the *Bondaweb* to make sure that you are using it the correct way up – the rough side goes next to the fabric.

2   Place the fabric face down on your ironing board, with the *Bondaweb* rough side next to the fabric. Iron it slowly and well to ensure good adhesion. Use the setting of the iron appropriate for the fabric. Allow to cool.

3   Draw strips onto the paper backing with a pencil and cut them out carefully. Peel the paper away from the fabric; you will be left with the glue on the wrong side of your fabric. Apply the same treatment to as many pieces of fabric as you need for the design.

4   Place the strips glue side down on the back of another piece of fabric, and iron them, using steam if possible. Allow to cool. If the strips do not stick well enough, iron again.

5   When all the strips are bonded on, either cover the raw edges with zigzag stitching, or use some other decorative stitching or pin-tucks to secure them.

75 Detail of the back of a kimono with strips cut into sections and bonded onto cream silk. (*Daphne Nicholson*)

76-78 Samples using bonded strips

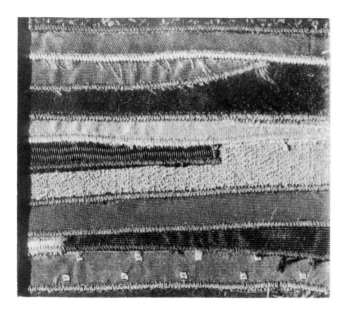

76 Part of the original piece showing bonded strips with the raw edges covered with close zigzag stitching. It was cut into three and this part was left without further decoration

77 *Above right* The second piece was cut into diagonal strips and bonded for a second time onto tartan fabric. The raw edges were covered with satin stitch

78 The third piece was also cut into diagonal strips and bonded onto tartan fabric, leaving wider spaces between the strips. These were stitched to form tucks and threaded through with quilting wool

Method 15 — Block patchwork using pre-stripped fabric

You can use a traditional block pattern or one you have designed yourself, and give it quite a different look by cutting some, or all, of the shapes from a fabric made by sewing strips of different fabrics together.

1 Draw your design on graph paper. Cut the shapes out carefully.

2 Glue the pieces to a piece of thin card or the smooth side of sandpaper, leaving spaces between for the seam allowances.

3 Measure and draw a line 6 mm (¼ in.) away from each edge of the graph paper shapes *(79a)*. Cut the templates out on these new lines, using a knife and metal ruler if possible.

4 Using method 1, sew strips of fabrics together to make a new fabric that is the same width as your template. (You might have to make a different striped fabric for each template). For a more varied effect, make the fabric wider than your templates, so that you can place the templates at random on them.

5 Place the templates on the pre-stripped fabric, according to the design. Mark all round the edges of the templates with a hard pencil or permanent pen. Carefully cut them out.

6 Pin and stitch each shape together as if you were using plain fabric, with 6 mm (¼ in.) seam allowance. Press seams open onto one side *(79b)*.

79 (a)

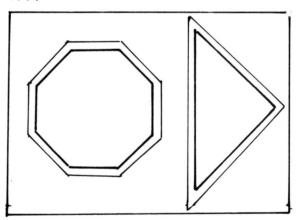

(b)

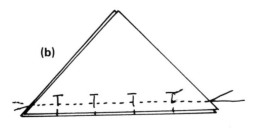

Octagon pattern
You can draft this pattern using a commercial octagonal template. Choose a fairly large one.

1 Place the octagon in the centre of a square that is about twice the width of the octagon *(80a)*.
2 Extend the lines from the edges of the octagon to the outside of the square *(80b)*.
3 Join up two of these points to make the corner triangle *(80c)*.
4 Make a triangular and an octagonal template, and another triangle for the corner piece, with

6 mm (¼ in.) seam allowance included.
5 Make a striped fabric to fit the larger triangle template.
6 Cut one octagon from plain fabric.
7 Place the larger triangle template on the pre-stripped fabric, draw round it and cut out eight shapes *(80d)*.
8 Join the triangles to the octagon in the order shown *(80e, f)*.
9 Add the corners to complete the pattern *(80g)*.

80

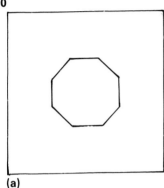

(a)

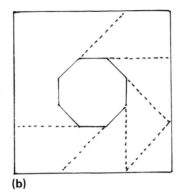

(b)

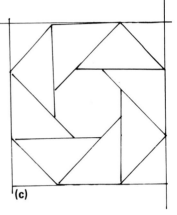

(c)

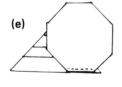

(e)

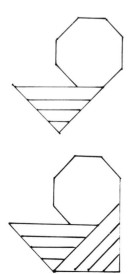

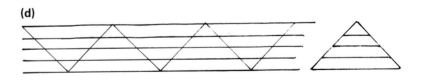

(d)

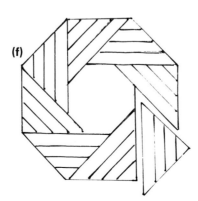

(f)

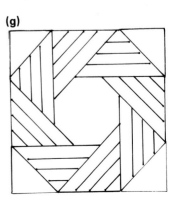

(g)

Patchwork Using Plain Strips

The technicalities of dyeing and the various sewing methods have been covered in the previous two chapters; the remaining sections will concentrate on designing for the different types of strip patchwork.

You may well want to begin with plain strips of fabric, in different proportions and colours. If the strips are wide the work grows very quickly, and you could make a quilt in a fortnight. If they are very narrow, then you need only make small pieces to decorate cushions and clothes designed to be seen at close quarters.

When using strips as the main decorative element, the most important aspects to consider are the colour and tone of the fabric and the proportion and direction of the stripes. Time and effort spent on solving design problems before you start will repay you many times over in satisfaction. A well thought-out piece of work will always be satisfying, whereas one begun too hastily is likely to leave problems unsolved, and you will continually notice where you went wrong. It is a good idea to make lots and lots of samples

to help you decide upon the best sewing method, the colour placing, the proportion of the stripes, and whether it looks better quilted or backed. When you have done all this you will have a much clearer idea of what you want the finished piece to look like, and so will be less likely to run into trouble. These samples are not wasted. They are part of the learning process and should be valued as such; sometimes they can even be made into small articles and given away as presents.

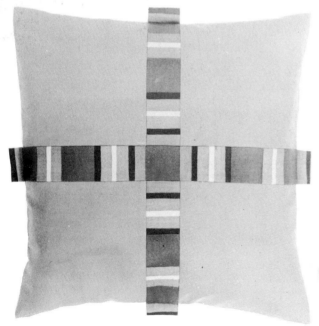

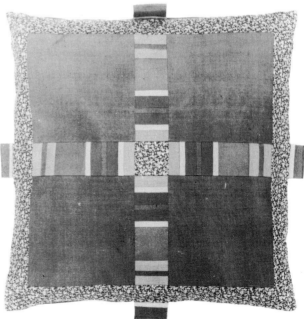

81 Consider these simple yet effective cushions. The proportion of the stripes, and of the plain to decorated areas, is perfect. The small tabs are just the right finishing touch. (*Andrea Statham*)

82 Cushion in four sections using
space-dyed fabrics. A mock-up of
the shape was made using calico
and cheap stuffing to get the correct
size and proportion. Then the strip
patchwork was made in colours that
become darker towards the bottom.
There is a rod along the centre to
keep the shape, and stuffed
rouleaux tie the shapes together
and form the tassels. (*Sarah
Balmain*)

83

Designs for square blocks

The designs on this page all have a square or a part-square set diamond-wise within the outer square, with some areas sub-divided into strips. You can use a block of your own design or a traditional one, and, by inserting strips into some parts of the block, give it a totally new look. To make these blocks, long strips should be sewn together first and the shapes cut from the pre-stripped fabric. This method saves a great deal of time, as sewing each shape individually to its neighbour would be very laborious. The strips must be sewn accurately so that the seams meet at the edges of the sections.

Designs using variations of traditional blocks

84 Line and tonal versions of traditional blocks with some areas divided into stripes

85 *Above left and left* A variation of the traditional baby block design, with added stripes

86 *Above* A block using stripes on the diagonal as well as vertically and horizontally. Some fabrics are space-dyed. (*Sarah Balmain*)

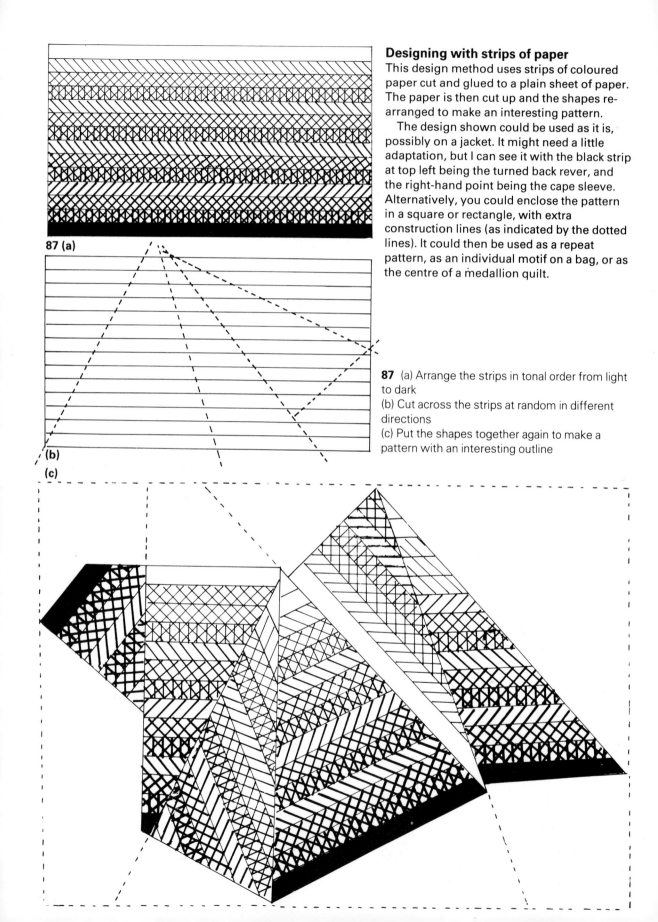

Designing with strips of paper

This design method uses strips of coloured paper cut and glued to a plain sheet of paper. The paper is then cut up and the shapes re-arranged to make an interesting pattern.

The design shown could be used as it is, possibly on a jacket. It might need a little adaptation, but I can see it with the black strip at top left being the turned back rever, and the right-hand point being the cape sleeve. Alternatively, you could enclose the pattern in a square or rectangle, with extra construction lines (as indicated by the dotted lines). It could then be used as a repeat pattern, as an individual motif on a bag, or as the centre of a medallion quilt.

87 (a)

(b)

(c)

87 (a) Arrange the strips in tonal order from light to dark
(b) Cut across the strips at random in different directions
(c) Put the shapes together again to make a pattern with an interesting outline

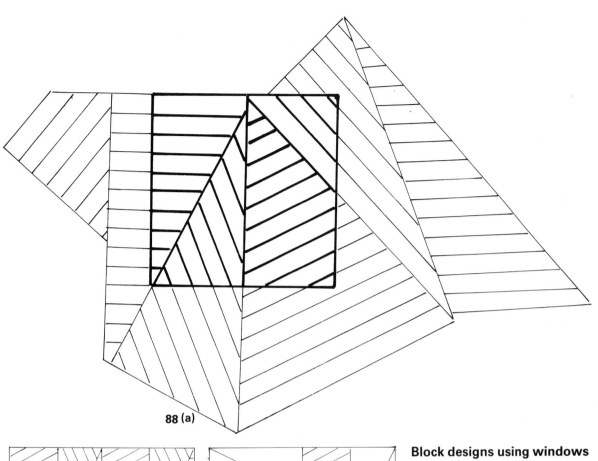

88 (a)

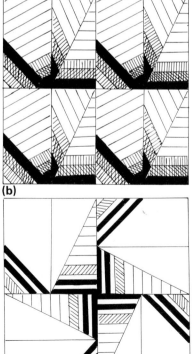

(b)

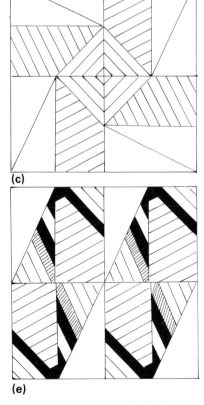

(c)

Block designs using windows
A square hole or window was cut in a piece of card and placed over the pattern to frame an interesting area. Windows can be of shapes other than squares, but these do not always fit together so easily.

(d)

(e)

88 (a) The pattern exposed in the window was traced to make a block design
(b) The block was drawn out as a repeat pattern with the shapes all facing the same way
(c), (d), (e) The same tracing was used for more designs, leaving out some of the stripes within the block. The blank areas could be of plain fabric. The direction of the block was changed in each of these patterns

Designing with cut paper shapes

Photocopies of mattress ticking were cut up into 38 mm (1½ in.) long diamonds and 38 mm (1½ in.) squares. These were glued to a drawing of an eight-point star to make patterns. The brief to the students was to consider the background shapes as of equal importance to the shapes within the star, and the final pattern was *not* to look like a star. You could colour the design in with felt-tip pen, and add extra lines across the plain areas.

When making the fabric blocks based on this design, sew strips of fabric together to correspond with the design, and place a card template on top as shown.

Mark and cut the fabric as in method 15 (page 62).

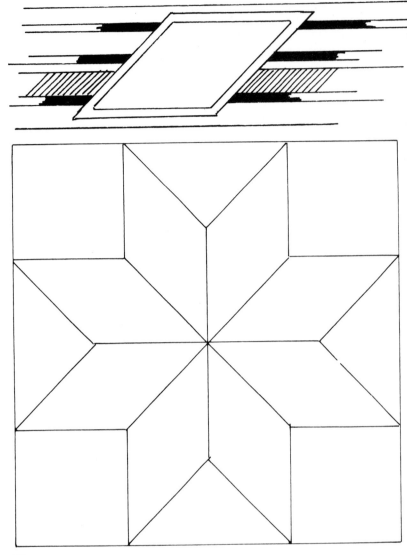

89

70

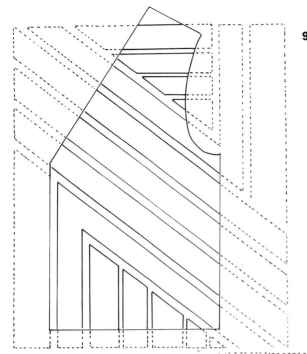

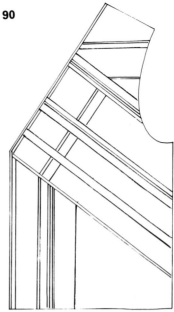

90

Designing simple clothes

A most satisfactory method of designing for any shape of garment is to cut a hole or window the shape of the finished garment and place it over a design, photograph or magazine illustration which incorporates strips. Move the window around until you have found the best position, which may be upside down or sideways. Then trace the exposed area. The basic lines can be added to, or taken away, and intricate details can be inserted into the seams to add texture.

All the windows illustrated were placed over the same painting, taken from a magazine.

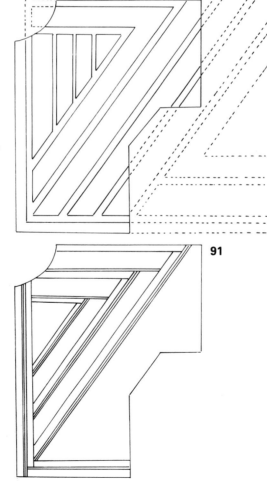

91

72

4 Quilt of plain and patterned
cottons. The coloured areas seem to
be behind the lattice pattern, and to
glow through it. (See chapter 9.)
(*Sheila Wells*)

5 A shaggy sheep made of numerous small pieces, sewn together in strips. A template was made for each shape — a fairly lengthy process. The wall hanging is quilted in a design of flowers and birds. (*Denise Orange*)

6 Jacket made from frayed strips of hand-dyed cottons. Some are plain colours and some are space-dyed. The strips are three layers of fabric thick, which gives six colours showing at each seam. (*Valerie Campbell-Harding*)

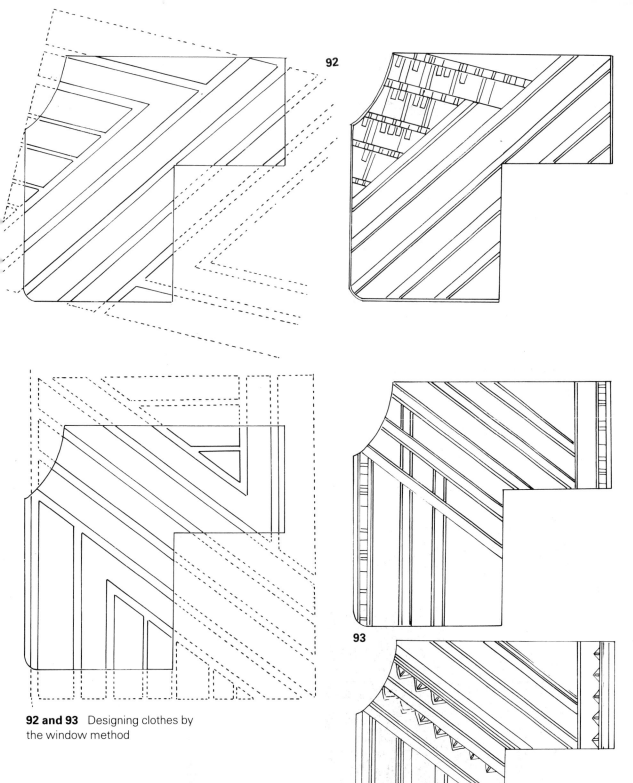

92 and 93 Designing clothes by
the window method

94 A drawing of Christmas wrapping paper in gold, wine, crimson, purple, blue and rust. The contrast between the width of the vertical bands, as well as the width of the strip between the bands, keeps one's interest. The arrow marks the repeat pattern

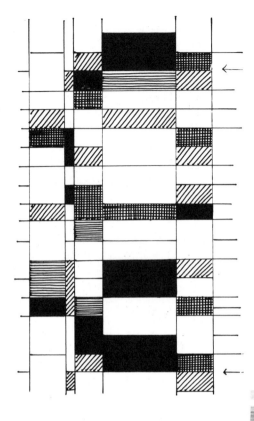

95 Here it is the tonal contrast which is interesting. Strip patchwork, laced over card, is placed on top of strips drawn with coloured pencils. In a finished piece of work the same contrast could be obtained by the use of light and dark coloured fabrics

Designing with striped paper

Either use Christmas wrapping paper, or make your own striped paper. Draw thick and thin lines with felt-tip pens of various colours on white or coloured paper. Keep the lines parallel by using a ruler, and completely cover the paper.

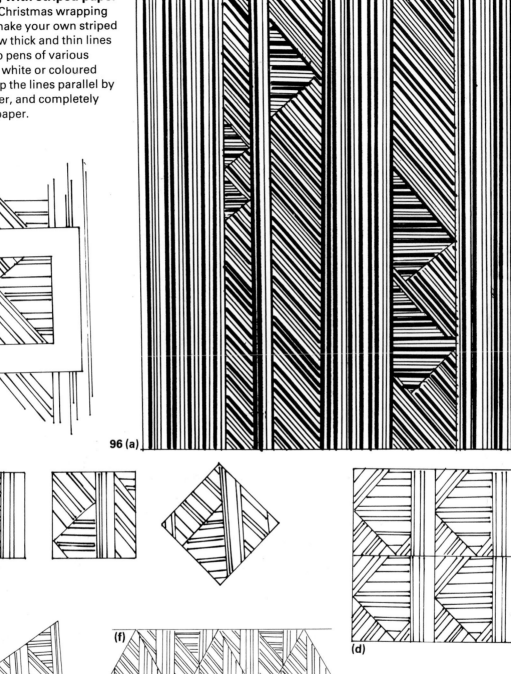

(b)

96 (a)

(c)

(e)

(f)

(d)

96 (a) Cut striped paper up into shapes and strips, and re-arrange these into a pleasing design. Have the stripes going in different directions. You can use this design as it is or take sections from it
(b) Cut a square hole in a piece of

card. Place this hole, or window, over the design and trace the exposed area
(c) Move the card around and trace a few more areas
(d) Choose the best and draw it as a repeat pattern. Colour it in the same

shades as the original paper, but perhaps making the stripes wider
(e) A triangluar window can be used
(f) A border pattern using the triangular block in two directions

75

Radiating strips

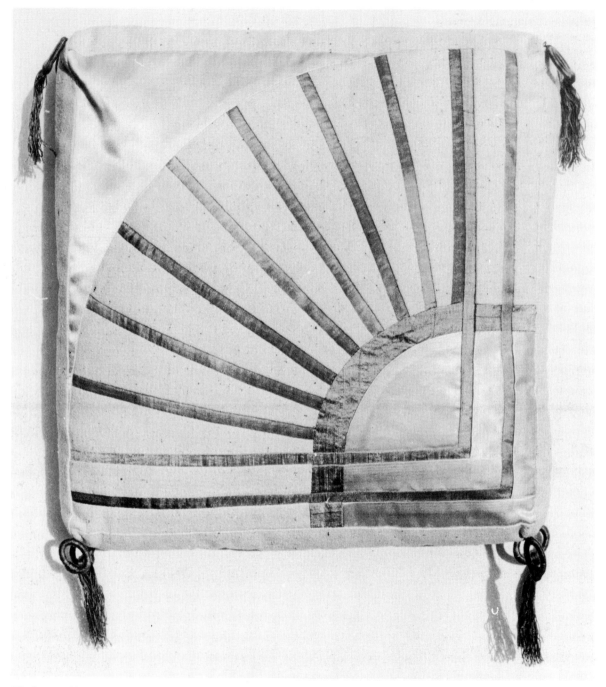

97 Fan cushion made using method 4 (sewing strips onto a background fabric). The whole design was drawn on calico using a hard pencil. Templates were made for the wedge shapes and corner pieces. These were cut from cream silks and satin. The main striped band was sewn first, using narrow strips of space-dyed silk between cream silk wedges. Then the corner pieces and strips were added, using the drawn lines as a guide to ensure accuracy. The tassels are made of silk threads space-dyed at the same time as the fabric. (*Valerie Campbell-Harding*)

Parallel strips

98 Cushion in silks and cottons, made using method 4 (page 42). The coloured fabrics are space-dyed, and frayed strips of the same fabrics are used as the tassels. Largely cream with rust, blue and wine. The idea for the shape of the cushion arose at a summer school when the brief given to the students was to alter the shape of a square cushion pad by pushing and pulling it. Here the opposite corners were drawn in and stitched right through the centre. (*Eunice Wells*)

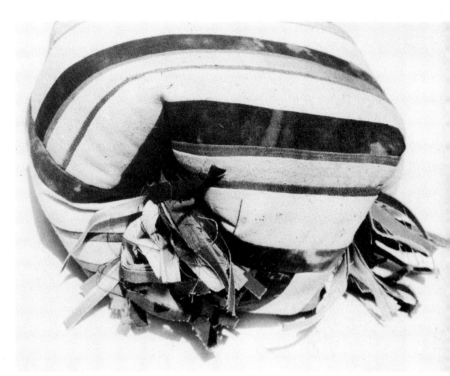

99 Table mat using bonded strips, in greys and yellows

100 A patriotic quilt in red, white and blue, to commemorate the Queen's Silver Jubilee. Notice how the flag design has been cut and used at random as a border. (*Deirdre Amsden. Photo: Dona Haycraft*)

101 *Opposite above* Four sides of a toy which appear as you turn it inside out. It is made by sewing 32 triangles of fabric-covered card together in four rows of eight triangles, using method 8 (paper-backed strips)

102 *Opposite* When all the triangles are sewn together, join A-A, B-B, C-C and D-D, oversewing the edges together on the wrong side. Then join E-E, F-F, G-G and so on, oversewing the edges together on the right side

101

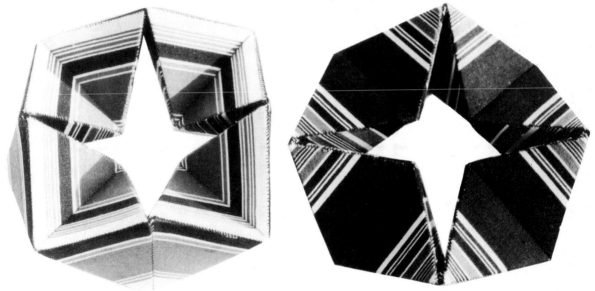

102

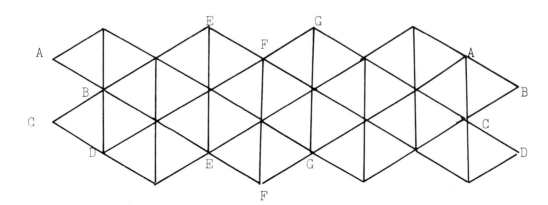

Stripes used as a background

The easiest way to translate the design illustrated would be to make up the whole area of fabric by sewing fabric strips together along their length, and then cut out and apply the figure shapes on top. This could be done by hand or machine. Lines of quilting echoing the edges of the applied shapes would bond all the layers together firmly. The stripes could be regular as here, or of varied widths. Interesting tonal or colour changes could take place across the design.

103

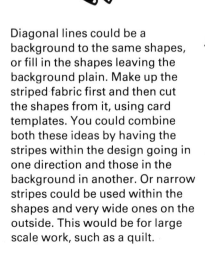

Diagonal lines could be a
background to the same shapes,
or fill in the shapes leaving the
background plain. Make up the
striped fabric first and then cut
the shapes from it, using card
templates. You could combine
both these ideas by having the
stripes within the design going in
one direction and those in the
background in another. Or narrow
stripes could be used within the
shapes and very wide ones on the
outside. This would be for large
scale work, such as a quilt.

5 Log Cabin Patchwork

104 (a)

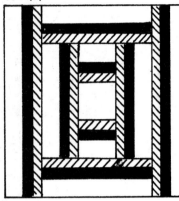

(b)

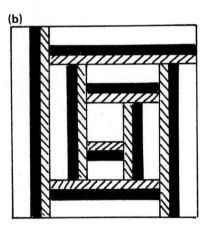

(c)

The strips in this form of patchwork represent the logs that make the walls of a log cabin. Traditionally the central square was red to suggest the warmth of the fire, and the dark side of the square represents the shadows cast by the fire. There are many variations of this much-loved pattern which can be made simply by concentrating on the dark and light tones of the fabric strips.

One variation can be made by sewing two or three strips of fabric together first, and then using these strips as a single strip around the central square, either in the spiral sewing sequence, or sewn as opposite pairs.

104 *Left* Pre-sewn strips around the central square:
(a) Courthouse steps sequence
(b) Spiral sequence
(c) A shaded pattern

106 *Right* Entirely different patterns emerge when the square is placed at the corner

107 Shading from dark to light in opposite directions within the same block gives a another pattern

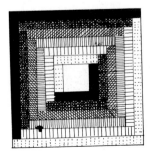

105 *Left* A traditional log cabin pattern, but with the central cross padded

(a)

108 (a) A log cabin quilt in cream, rust, browns, blue and black. A greater variety of tone is achieved by covering some of the blocks with either one or two layers of black net. (*Valerie Campbell-Harding*)
(b) Detail of the quilt

(b)

Folded centres for log cabin

Although it is usual to have plain squares or other shapes as the centre of log cabin blocks, if you enlarge the central square you can add different patterns, folded shapes, embroidered centres, other patchwork methods or tucks and pleats.

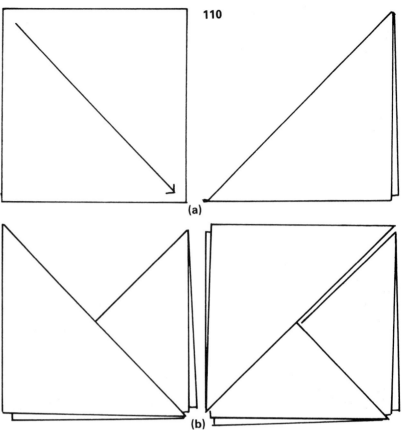

110

(a)

(b)

(c)

109 A block with a central square of folded triangles, using striped fabric

110 (a) A square of fabric is folded in half diagonally. Fold three more squares in the same way
(b) Place the second on top of the first as shown, and then the third on top of the second
(c) Place the fourth on top of the third and under the first

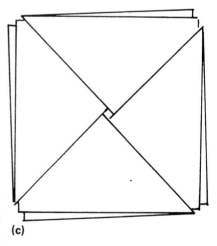

111 In this cushion a more complicated pattern has been built up using folded triangles, and log cabin strips make a border. Silks, satin, organza and cotton, using plain and space-dyed fabrics in pinks and mauves. (*Valerie Campbell-Harding*)

Embroidered centres for log cabin

113 Detail of one of the squares

112 Cushion of log cabin squares, each one with a different embroidery at the centre. Fine machine embroidery echoes the floral feeling in the fabrics used for the patchwork. (*Elizabeth Heitzmann*)

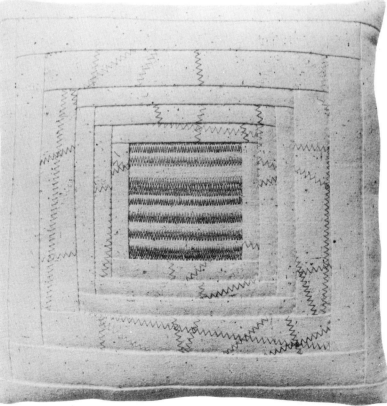

114 Silk cushion with lines of coloured stitching, dense at the centre and more open on the strips. (*Valerie Campbell-Harding*)

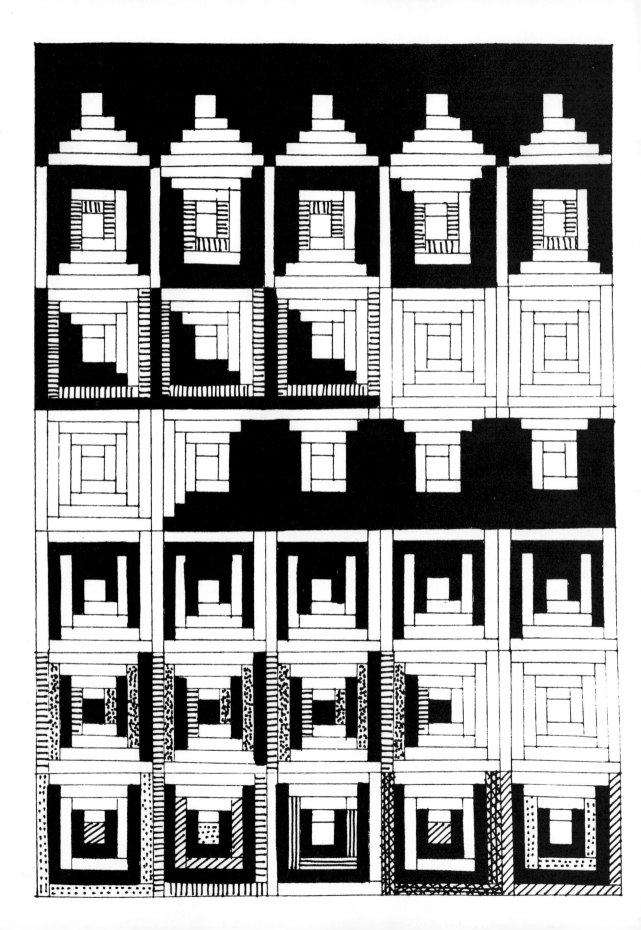

115 *Opposite* Suggestions for borders using log cabin blocks. Most of these are best made up using the courthouse steps method of construction, adding the strips in opposite pairs

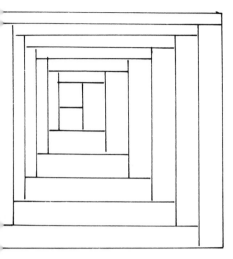

116 *Above* A block with all the thin strips on one side and the thick ones on the other

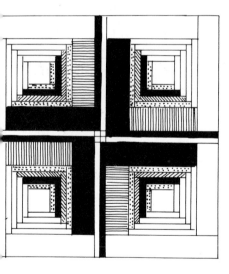

117 *Above* Four blocks put together. The thick strips on the outside of the black block keep the pattern contained within a border

Using thick and thin strips

Using two widths together can give a distinctly curved look to a pattern and this can be emphasized by quilting in curves afterwards. The central shape can be square or rectangular; this shape can also be positioned at one corner or on one side of the block, instead of in the centre. The thin strips could be used to introduce small amounts of contrasting colour next to the thicker strips. The sequence of construction is the same as for ordinary log cabin, but be sure to add more thin strips on one side to make the design even, or you will end up with a square or rectangle which is not central.

118 Silk cushion using thin and thick stripes around a central square of pin-tucked appliqué. Sprayed and dyed silks. (*Valerie Campbell-Harding*)

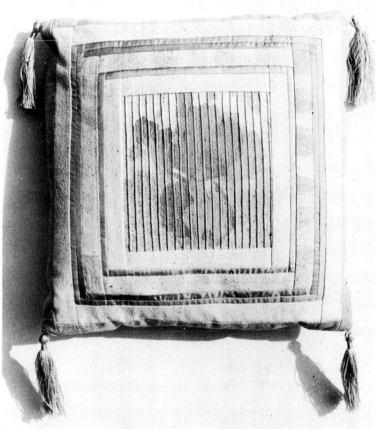

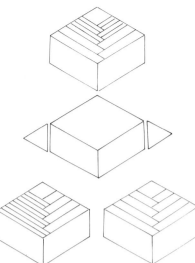

Log cabin within triangles and diamonds

These designs are perfectly simple to piece using methods 6 or 7 (pages 46, 48). Remember to cut the strips of fabric quite a bit longer than you would think necessary, to ensure that they overlap at the points.

The triangle and diamond blocks are easy to machine-sew together, but the baby block variation will need either small triangles at the corners, or careful stitching at the angles.

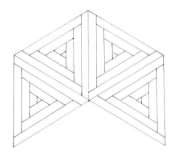

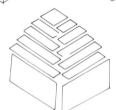

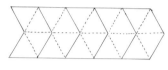

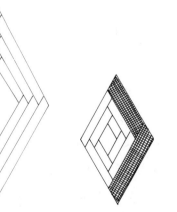

119 Triangle blocks

120 *Below* Diamond blocks

121 *Above* Baby block variation

122 *Above* Triangle log cabin

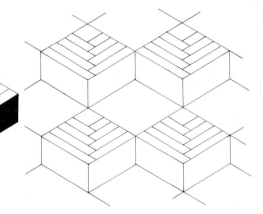

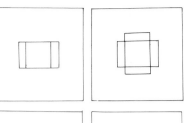

123 A method of building up the pineapple pattern using strips sewn to a backing

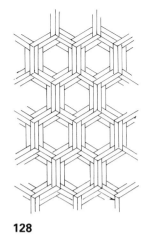

127

129

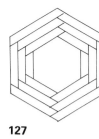

124 Completed block shading from dark to light

Log cabin within hexagons and octagons

Log cabin strips are an interesting way of breaking up these shapes. Hexagons will fit together to make all-over patterns, but octagons will not. Triangles are therefore added at the corners to make a square block which will fit with its neighbour. This is called the pineapple pattern, and can be constructed using strips as shown in the diagram. Be careful not to overlap the strips at the ends, as this will result in too much bulk.

127 Strips sewn around a central hexagon

128 A number of hexagons sewn together. The colouring can vary throughout the pattern to break up the absolute regularity

129 Raffia pile cloth from the Congo. Patterns like this suggest new ways of using log cabin patchwork, perhaps with two different blocks together

125 Four pineapple blocks together

126 *Right* Single pineapple block

Log cabin on the diagonal

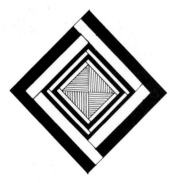

130 Block designs suggested by the pile cloth pattern (*129*). Tabs can be added for cushion and bag edges

131 Cream silk cushion with log cabin strips around a central square of pintucks (*Valerie Campbell-Harding*)

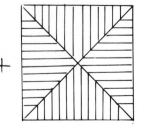

132 *Below* Squares of strips or pintucks can be cut up to make patterns with the strips or tucks going in different directions. Do not forget to allow for the 6 mm (¼ in.) seam allowance, although this will not matter if you are going to add further strips around the outside edge

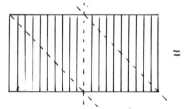

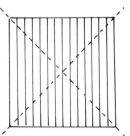

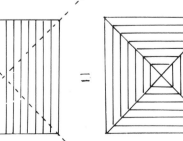

V-shaped patterns

These can be made using only two sides of the log cabin block, with either flat or folded strips (methods 6, 7, or 10, pages 46, 48, 54).

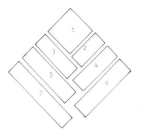

133 The sequence of construction, whatever the final shape

134 Narrow strips on one side and wide on the other make an interesting contrast

135 Bag made of hand-dyed cottons using thin and thick strips in blues, pinks, purples and rusts. (*Valerie Campbell-Harding*)

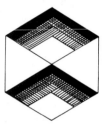

136

136 *Above right* V-shapes can fill in many other shapes such as hexagons, diamonds, tilted squares, ovals or circles. Here the stripes are of equal width

137 *Left* Tie made from hand-dyed cotton using thin and thick strips in the proportion of 1-4 in navy, blues and rusts. (*Eunice Wells*)

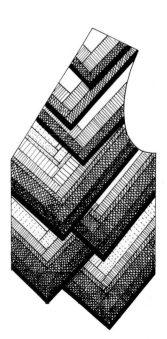

138 Design for a waistcoat using stripes in the proportions of 3-2-1. The whole garment is made of bound flaps laid on top of each other

Spiral patterns

The spiral motif is of great antiquity and almost universal. It can be found in abundance in the arts of Mexico, Chile, Peru, China, Japan and Greece. It was used in Britain by the Celts, in New Zealand by the Maoris, and also in New Guinea, the Congo and Nigeria. The combinations and proportions vary, but nearly all spirals are best put together using the log cabin method with a slightly altered sequence of construction.

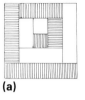 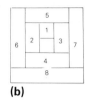

(a)   **(b)**

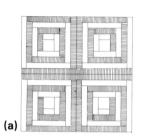

(a)

139 (a) Simple block pattern with strips sewn to a central square
(b) The sewing sequence for (a)

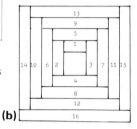

140 (a) Four slightly different blocks put together to give a more intricate pattern
(b) The sewing sequence for (a)   **(b)**

142 suggestions for other spiral patterns

141 Fabric block using contrasting colours to show the pattern

Variations on the standard log cabin block

143 A line has been drawn right through the block in the top left diagram. The pattern has been coloured in the top central diagram. When sewing a block like this the strips would have to be pieced first, and then attached as usual to the central square, matching the seams. The diagram at the top right is a variation with a second line dividing the block still further. Other variations are shown underneath

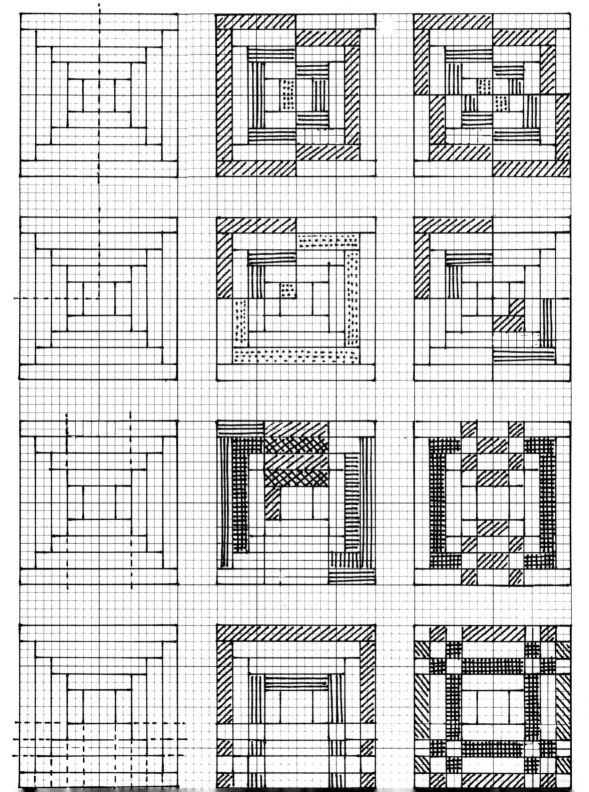

144 (a) Log cabin panel using different sections and both sides of a printed fabric. Strips were bonded to a backing using method 14, and machine embroidery in fine gold and coloured threads was added. Narrow black ribbons were laid over the top to hold the cords in place. Squares of card were covered in black moiré and wrapped with twisted threads. There is a colour change from top to bottom of the panel, both in the fabric strips and the wrapping. (*Valerie Campbell-Harding*)
(b) Detail of the panel

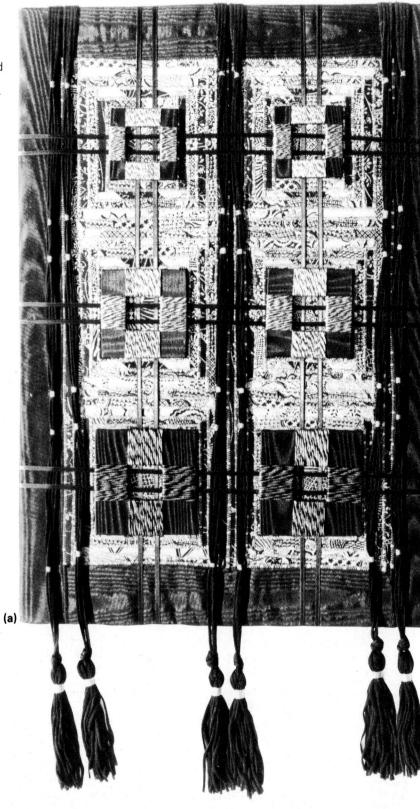

(a)

Strips of Patterns

The Seminole Indians of Florida developed a method of making intricate patterns by sewing together long strips of different widths, then cutting them across the seams and re-seaming the sections together in different ways. The cuts can be straight or at an angle, and the sections can be reversed or staggered, or sections of different bands can be sewn together. Traditionally these patterns were tiny and used to decorate clothing. From this developed the idea of cutting shapes apart from strips out of the pattern bands to build up patchwork more quickly than by piecing each individual shape to its neighbour. This means that you can use very tiny shapes, sometimes only 6 mm (¼ in.) across, in your pattern, which would be virtually impossible by any other method.

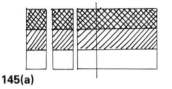

145(a)

146(a)

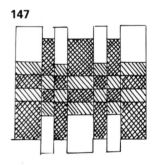

(c)

147

(b)

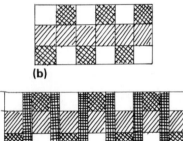

(b)

(c)

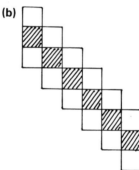

145 (a) A simple pattern cut into strips to make squares
(b) The strips are reversed and sewn together again
(c) A strip of plain fabric inserted between the pattern strips

146 Staggered strips sewn together to make diamonds

147 A more intricate pattern

148 Tea cosy made using the pattern shown above between strips of plain colours. (*Valerie Campbell-Harding*)

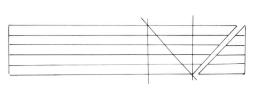

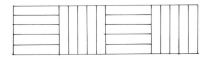
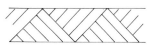

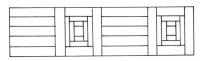
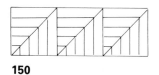

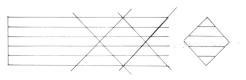

149

150

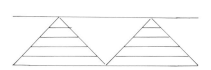

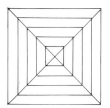
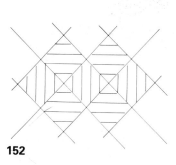

Patterns from pre-stripped fabric

Some of the patterns that can be made by cutting a pre-stripped fabric in different ways and sewing the cut pieces together again at different angles are shown here. The cuts can be straight or on the diagonal. The width of the strips making up the fabric can vary, and so can the colours. These blocks and borders can be sewn to each other, to different patterns, or to plain fabric. The patterns can be simple or intricate, but this method saves a great deal of time. The original strips must be sewn together very accurately or they will not meet at the seams when re-joined.

151

152

153

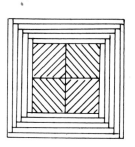

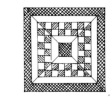

156

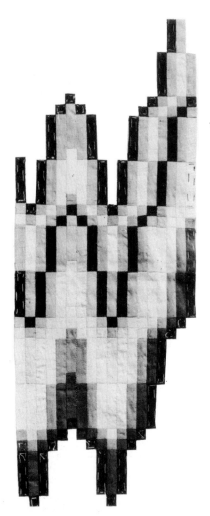

Shapes in strips

Simple shapes can be sewn together in long strips, and when the strips are joined new patterns emerge. One of the best known of these is the Japanese tortoiseshell pattern made from half hexagons. The resulting fabric has here been made into kimonos. This is really the only way of making hexagons by machine, and if the colours on each side of a seam are the same, the join is not very noticeable.

158 *Opposite above* (a) Kimono made using the Japanese tortoiseshell pattern
(b) Method of constructing the strips
(c), (d) Other patterns made from the same strips

159 *Opposite* (a) Triangles put together in long strips to make diamond patterns
(b), (c) Variations of (a)

154 *Left* Part of a quilt with a design of cut and shifted stripes, using slub silks in creams, pinks, wine and black

155 (a)-(c) A band built up by sewing plain strips to each side of the patterned strip
(d) Triangles are cut from the band so that no material is wasted

156 *Above* Three possible designs using the triangles

157 *Below right* Waistcoat using this pattern band together with others

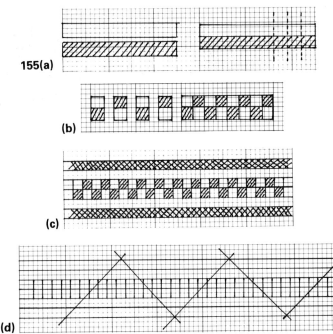

155(a)

(b)

(c)

(d)

160 *Below right* A cushion in shot silk made by sewing half hexagons together in strips. (*Valerie Campbell-Harding*)

161 *Bottom right* (a) To construct flaps and turned shapes, place two pieces of fabric together, face to face. Draw the shape on the top, exactly the size you wish it to be at the finish. Stitch on three sides. Trim excess fabric away, leaving about 6 mm
(¼ in.) all round the shape. Turn inside out and press
(b) The finished shapes inserted into a seam

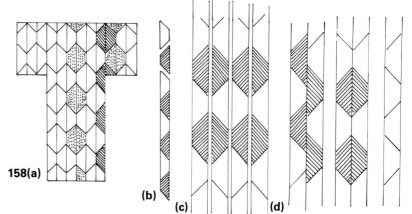

158(a)

(b)

(c)

(d)

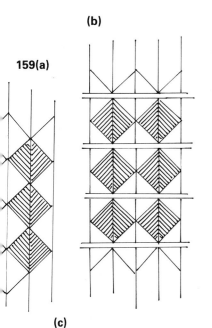

(b)

159(a)

(c)

160

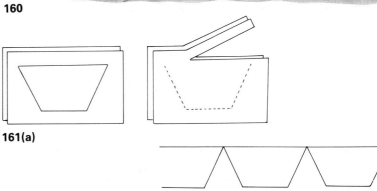

161(a)

(b)

162 *Left* A waistcoat of silk noil in cream, dusty pink, gentle yellow ochres, and pale purple-blues. The pattern on the front was sprayed onto the silk with car spray paint, carefully matching the colours of the patchwork at the sides. Hand quilting and embroidery were added, using space-dyed threads, and tassels from the same threads. (*Valeria Campbell-Harding*)

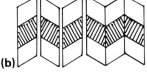

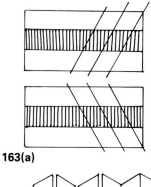

163(a)

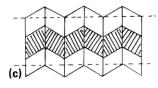

(b)

(c)

Chevron patterns

Chevron patterns can be made by sewing strips of fabric together and cutting strips from them at two different angles. These strips are sewn together alternately and the points are trimmed off to leave a straight band.

163 *Left* (a) The straight lines indicate the cutting lines which are at 45°
(b) The strips placed alternately
(c) The strips sewn together and trimmed

165 *Above* Chevron pattern using method 15 (vilene-backed strips) (page 62)

164 *Left* Detail of the chevron pattern at the sides of the waistcoat *(162)*. The proportion of the strips is 3-1-1, and this proportion is repeated in the sprayed chevrons on the front of the waistcoat

166 *Below* Designs for chevrons using strips of different widths and angles

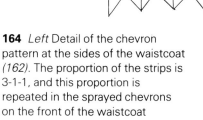

Diamonds and triangles

167 (a) Strips of fabric are sewn together to make a new, patterned fabric. It is cut into shapes which are then sewn together to make a different pattern. The dotted lines indicate the cutting lines. Include 6 mm (¼ in.) seam allowance on all edges of each shape
(b) The shapes are seamed together in the order D, C, B, A and so on

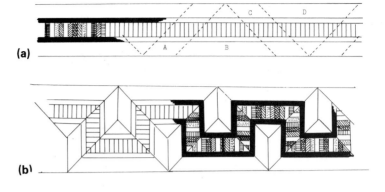

168 The finished border using plain and printed cottons in blues, purples, greens and black. (*Sheila Wells*)

169 Star block pattern
(a) The block pattern with extra seam lines added for ease of sewing. These are shown by the dotted lines
(b) The diamonds that make up the stars are cut from pre-stripped fabric
(c) Two sizes of triangle are needed to fill in the background, and the pieces are sewn together in this sequence
(d) The completed pattern. The background areas could also be stripped

169

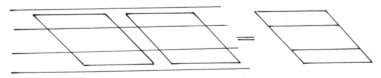

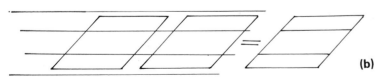

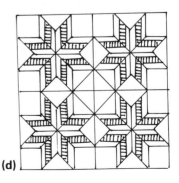

7 Curved Strips

A design with curved strips has more movement in it than one with straight lines only, and curves are not necessarily more difficult to sew. Shallow curves are quite easy, but it is better to avoid sharp ones and particularly U-shapes. The simplest way to design for curved strip patchwork is to keep to the concept of the repeating square block. You can draw the curves free-hand, trace them or use a pair of compasses. The strips can be of equal or unequal width and need not be parallel to each other. Blocks from different designs can be used together but geometric curves and freely drawn curves do not usually mix well.

170 Wall hanging in shades of pink using hand-dyed fabrics. The design was drawn with compasses, and the quilting lines echo the seam lines. (*Pamela Watts*)

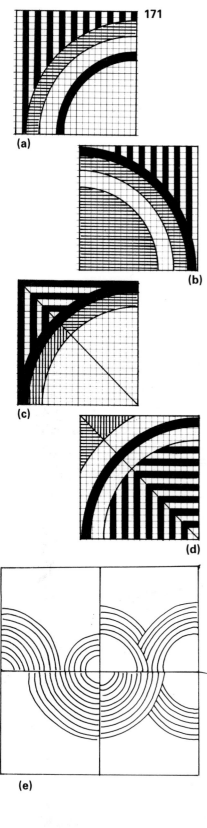

(a)

(b)

(c)

(d)

(e)

Patterns using quarter circles

The patterns on this page illustrate the use of a quarter circle in one corner of a square. An effective way to colour in these patterns, which helps to break up the regularity of the geometrically drawn curves, is to trace the whole pattern using good quality tracing paper (not greaseproof). Then place the tracing over a coloured

171 (a)-(d) Each design shows a different-sized quarter circle with added curves and straight strips (e) A pattern using the quarter circles. Some of the blocks have curves in two directions. These are sewn by making up one section of curves first, and then piecing it to the second section as if they were plain fabric

photograph with interesting areas of colour, and colour your pattern in with coloured pencils in the same places. Do not worry if the colour does not quite fit in with the shapes in the blocks. You can either piece some of the curved strips first to make them two or three colours within a band, or you can fill in each area with a separate colour which approximates with that on the photograph but is not in exactly the same place.

172 *Below* Design for a whole quilt using quarter circles. These are placed in different directions to give movement to the design, and some blocks are left empty in contrast. The widths of the stripes within each block vary

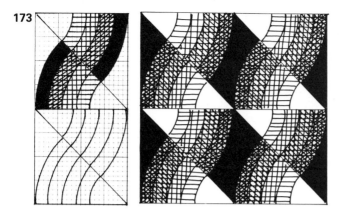

173

Shallow curves

Shallow curves are easier to piece than sharper ones, and you can draw them with a pair of compasses or by using a large plate as a pattern. To get an S-shape, draw the curves in half the square only. Trace this half, flip the tracing paper over and draw the same curves in the other half (*173*).

174 Part of a quilt using this pattern, which gives a strong sense of a receding landscape. (*Sarah Balmain*)

Design ideas

Look at skies, seas or landscapes and draw the wavy lines that you see. Colour them in tonal order from light to dark, or use the colour sequence in the landscape. This could be from the blue of the sky, through the greens and golds of the fields, the darker greens and brown of the hedgerows, to the dark murky colours of the earth and roots.

Make up a piece of patchwork in the same colours as the design. Then cut it into three or more vertical strips. Reverse alternate strips and sew them together again (*175*). You could insert a piece of plain fabric between the pieced strips.

A design source frequently overlooked is an existing piece of patchwork.

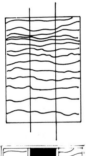
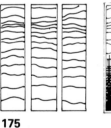
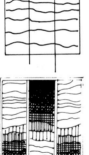

175

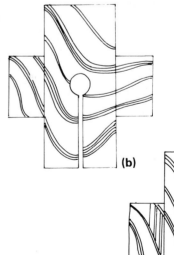

176 Sample using method 13 (vilene-backed strips) (page 58)

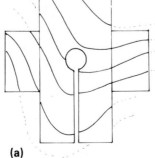

177 (a) A jacket pattern was traced onto a piece of paper and placed over the sample at a slight angle. The lines were traced onto the jacket pattern
(b) Extra lines were added for interest
(c) Some of the areas were further divided with straight lines. These would be narrow strips which would be pieced first

(a)

(b)

(c)

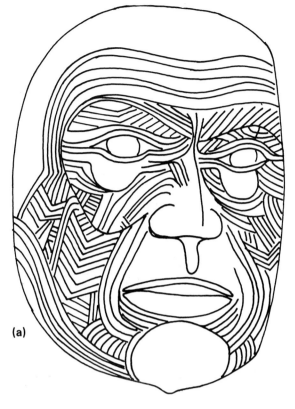

(a)

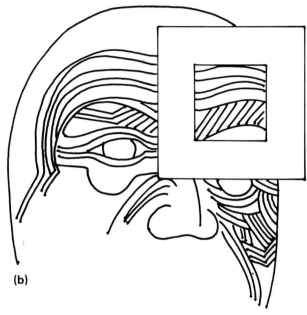

(b)

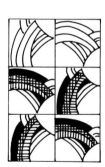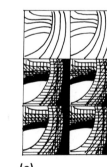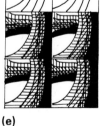 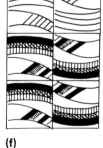

(c)

(d)

(e)

(f)

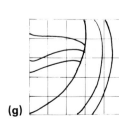

(g)

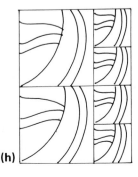

(h)

178(a) A Tsimshian carved wooden mask. A stylized representation of an old man with bags under his eyes and wrinkled skin

(b) Place a square window over parts of the drawing

(c) Trace the exposed pattern, move the window and trace another one. Do several so that you can choose the best

(d)-(f) Draw the patterns as repeats and fill in with colour or tone to give an idea of the final result. As the original carved mask has no colour scheme to use, I suggest that you look closely at a flower or piece of fruit and use the colours visible there

(g) Enlarge the pattern by the grid method, dividing the original block into a given number of squares. Draw a second, larger square and divide it into the same number of small squares. Copy the pattern lines free-hand into the larger design, square by square

(h) The two sizes of square can be used together

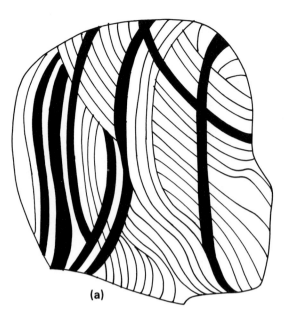

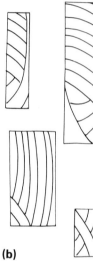
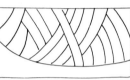
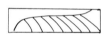
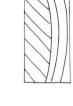

(b)

179 Block patterns from windows
placed over photographs
(a) A tracing of a photograph of a
wig stand onto which a slide of
stripes was projected
(b) Rectangular windows were
placed over the drawing and the
exposed area traced
(c) One pattern repeated, facing in
two directions
(d) Another pattern, also facing in
two directions
(e) Long, narrow shapes suggesting
borders
(f) Two rectangles of different
proportions placed next to each
other to make a single block. This
gives the effect of shapes appearing
from behind

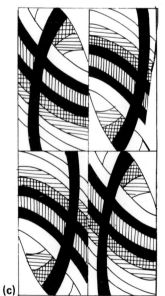
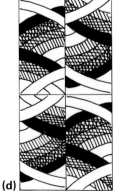

(c) **(d)** **(e)** **(f)**

Using colour

The first two illustrations on this page are block patterns produced by placing windows over drawings and paintings. Colours were picked at random from a box of felt-tip pens, using as many colours as there were shapes in each block. They were arranged in tonal order from light to dark and the design was coloured in the same order, starting from one edge or one corner of each block. It is not easy to tell the tonal order from the outside of the pens and you have to test them on a piece of paper. Some surprising and interesting colour schemes appear using the method, and it does help you to break away from your usual choice. Do not despair if your choice seems dreadful. For the second pattern you could remove one of the colours and choose a new one. The more you push your colour sense and the more unusual combinations you try, the more interesting your choice will become.

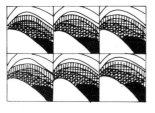
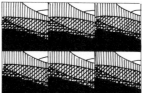

180 Design based on a shell

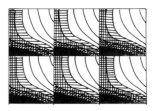
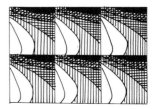

181 Patterns derived from paintings

182 (a) A design using the letter N. Tracings were made of the letter, moving the tracing paper each time. A window was placed over part of the pattern

(b) The letter shapes were filled in with lines of different widths. The design would have to be enlarged to a reasonable size. Strip patchwork can be made up as a whole fabric, the shapes cut from it and applied to a plain colour; or each shape can be pieced separately. Some extra seams will have to be added if you use this method. (*Daphne Nicholson*)

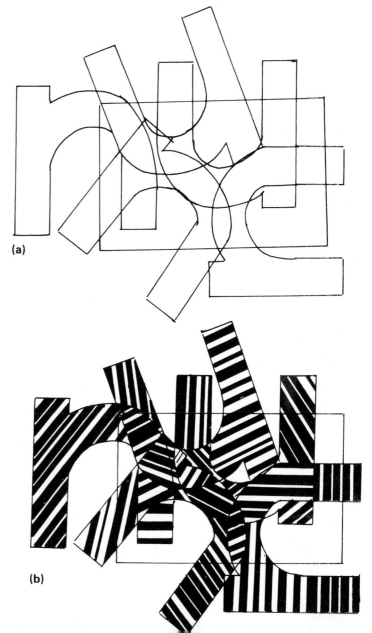

(a)

(b)

Textured Strips

Strip patchwork can often be made more interesting by the addition of texture, and there are many ways of doing this. The seams need not be hidden but can be on the front of the work with frayed or embroidered edges. Bound or French seams in another colour can be left showing. Flaps, folded pieces of fabric, turned shapes or piping can be inserted into some of the seams. The strips themselves can be pleated or folded before being sewn to each other, and torn strips can be knitted or crocheted as a contrast to the plain areas.

If you choose to introduce texture, keep the colour scheme simple, or the work will become too busy. Textured patchwork has the added advantage of not requiring quilting, as there will be enough body to the fabric already.

183(a)

183 (a) Cushion made of mattress
ticking which was pleated, frayed,
applied with ribbon, embroidered,
and then sewn together in strips in
tonal sequence from dark at one
side of the cushion to light at the
other. Gold thread was added to
give warmth to the colour scheme,
and the tassels also included gold.
(*Valerie Campbell-Harding*)
(b) Detail of the cushion

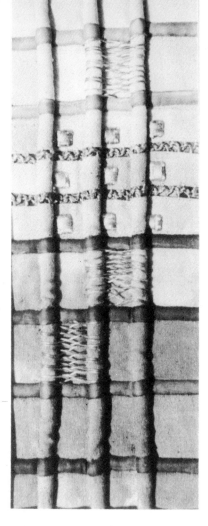

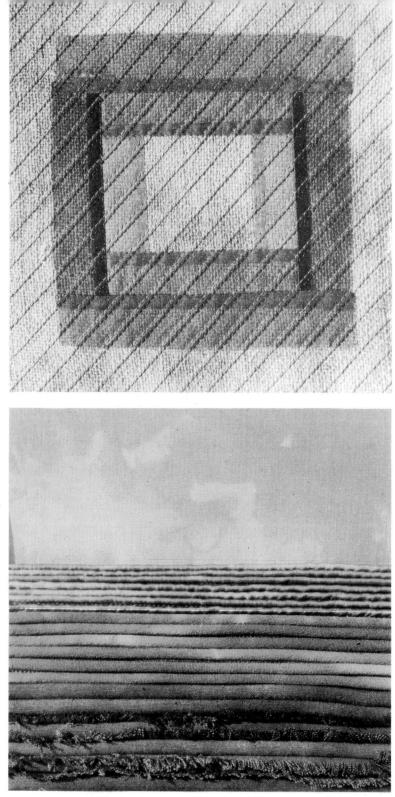

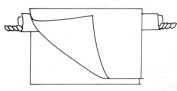

184 *Above left* Pin tucking across log cabin patchwork to give added body and to hold the organza strips firmly to the backing, which is of space-dyed fabric

185 *Above right* Strip patchwork made by method 4 (strips sewn to a fabric backing) (page 42) which was then pleated over piping cord and stitched. Some of the strips were joined using insertion stitches instead of seaming, and hand embroidery was added afterwards

186 *Left* Rows of piping using space-dyed fabrics from pale to dark. Frayed strips were inserted into some of the seams

184-187 Piping and tucking to give texture

187 *Far left* Method of inserting piping into a seam

188 Wall hanging using knitted strips of fabric surrounded by log cabin patchwork. The fabric is hand-dyed cotton in shades of pink from wine to almost cream. (*Pamela Watts*)

189 Kimono completely covered with frayed strips in white, red, purple and black. Each strip is sewn to the backing with a line of satin stitch along the centre. The design is taken from a drawing of tubes of paint in a box as shown on the design sheet at bottom left. The design sheet at bottom right is a tissue paper mock-up of a waistcoat to be made up using strips of silk joined with insertion stitches. (*Margaret Rivers*)

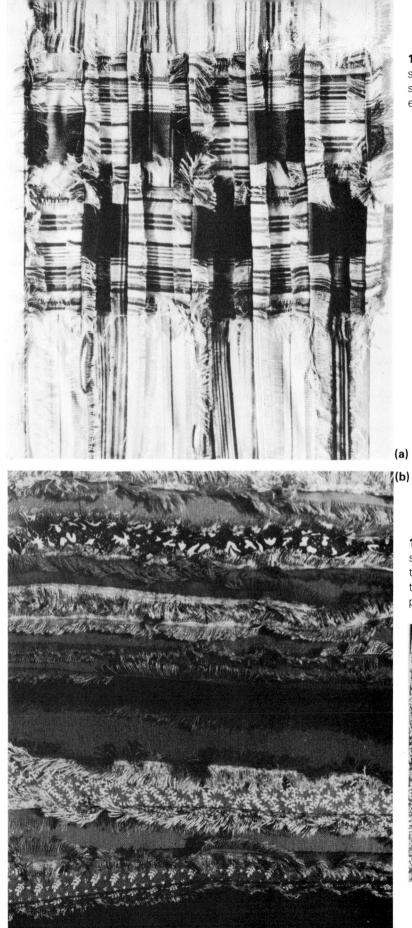

(a)

(b)

190 (a) and (b) Strips of fabric stitched to each other with the seams on the right side, and the edges of the seams frayed

191 *Below* Log cabin block with the seams at the front, frayed back to the stitching. It has been quilted, so the texture is very rich but still practical

192 Detail of a jacket made from frayed strips of fabric, with the seams on the right side. There are three layers of fabric throughout, with six colours showing at each seam. Some space-dyed fabrics were used, with plain hand-dyed ones to match, in blues and tawny-golds. The stripes were torn 5 cm (2 in.) wide, with the narrower strips at the seams giving enough variation. See colour plate 6. (*Valerie Campbell-Harding*)

193 Sample showing frayed strips

194 Waistcoat made of pleated strips as in method 11 (page 56), using space-dyed silk and cotton fabrics. Cords of space-dyed yarns, wrapped at intervals, are held to the waistcoat with tiny buttonhole loops. An applied and embroidered flower is added to the lining to add interest to the inside of the garment. (*Valerie Campbell-Harding*)

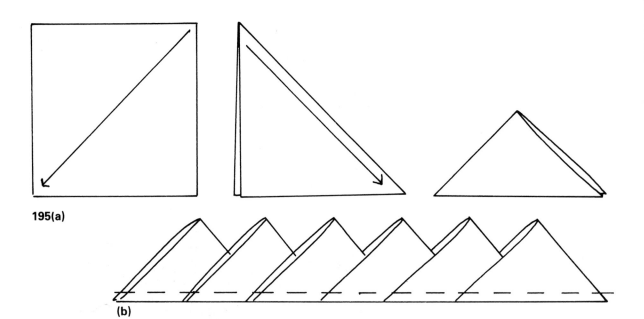

195(a)

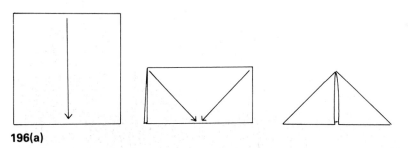

(b)

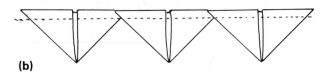

196(a)

(b)

(c)

195-196 Two methods of folding squares for insertion into seams to give texture and pattern

195 (a) Cut 5 cm (2 in.) squares of fabric. Fold in half on the diagonal, and again in half on the diagonal
(b) Slip the folded side of each triangle into the open side of the next one, and tack along the raw edges at the bottom

196 (a) The fabric square is folded in half horizontally. Bring the top corners of the fold to the centre of the raw edges at the bottom
(b) Slightly overlap the triangles and tack in a strip of the required length
(c) Folded triangles included in a seam

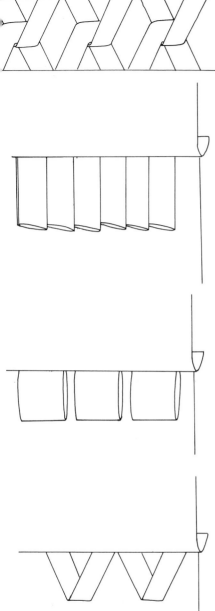

197 Diagrams of various inserted flaps, pleats, folded strips and rouleaux. They can be padded, lined with a different colour or embroidered to add interest

198 Detail of cushion with satellites, shown in colour plate 2. Folded triangles have been inserted in the seams to lie on the wider strips. (*Valerie Campbell-Harding*)

199 (a) Waistcoat made from
mattress ticking lined with flowered
cotton. The strips of ticking have
been embroidered and applied with
ribbons to give tonal gradation from
dark at the bottom to lighter at the
shoulders. Woven strips, flaps and
folded triangles have been inserted
into the seams to give texture.
(*Valerie Campbell-Harding*)
(b) Detail of the waistcoat

200 Fitted waistcoat using red and white striped and checked fabrics. Many different methods of pleating and tucking, turned shapes, woven fabric strips, flaps and triangles have been included, and the result is very exuberant. (*Clare Paterson*)

Woven and Interlaced Patterns

These patterns can be made either by actually weaving strips of fabric to give texture and firmness, or by piecing them to look like weaving, but with less bulk. For ideas for patterns look at woven fabrics or weaving books with diagrams of the different weaves. Baskets, chair seats and fences are all fruitful sources of patterns.

Twisted and interlaced patterns are common to many civilizations and they are frequent among Celtic and Viking designs, in ancient Mexican and Islamic art,

and in central Africa, China and Japan. Many of them seem complicated, but if you study a pattern carefully you can often find a simple repeat that builds up to the final result simply by including extra strips or squares between the blocks.

Simple weaving patterns can be made by the weaving of fabric strips in different colours, either with frayed edges, or by making sewn fabric strips. The most satisfactory methods I have found of doing this (*201*) are:

1 By turning the raw edges over

at each side and top-stitching the fold, as in the ticking cushion. This means that you can see what you are doing and can put a woven stripe in the fabric right on the edge of the fold.

2 By folding a strip of fabric in half lengthways and stitching it 6 mm (¼ in.) from the raw edges. This strip can be turned inside out. However, I have found that it is better not to do this but to leave the seam on the outside, pressed open, down the centre of the strip. This avoids a bump on the front.

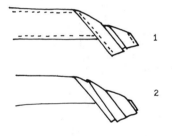

201

202, 203 Two cushions illustrating weaving patterns (*Valerie Campbell-Harding*)

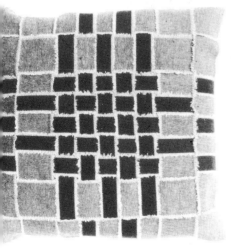

204 Cushion of woven strips using space-dyed silk and cotton fabrics. The texture is more interesting than if pieced squares were used, and weaving is also much quicker to work. The border is pieced according to method 4 (page 42), with extra strips laid on top of the fabric to integrate it with the central area. (*Eunice Wells*)

205 *Opposite* (a)-(e) The sequence of construction for a pieced pattern. Joining in the central square is the only difficult stage. Stitch from x to x only, leaving the rest of the seam open. Add the other shapes in a clockwise sequence, finally stitching from x to y (f), (g) Variations of the pattern

206 *Opposite* Four patterns drawn while looking at woven fabric through a magnifying glass. They can be pieced in the same way as the first pattern

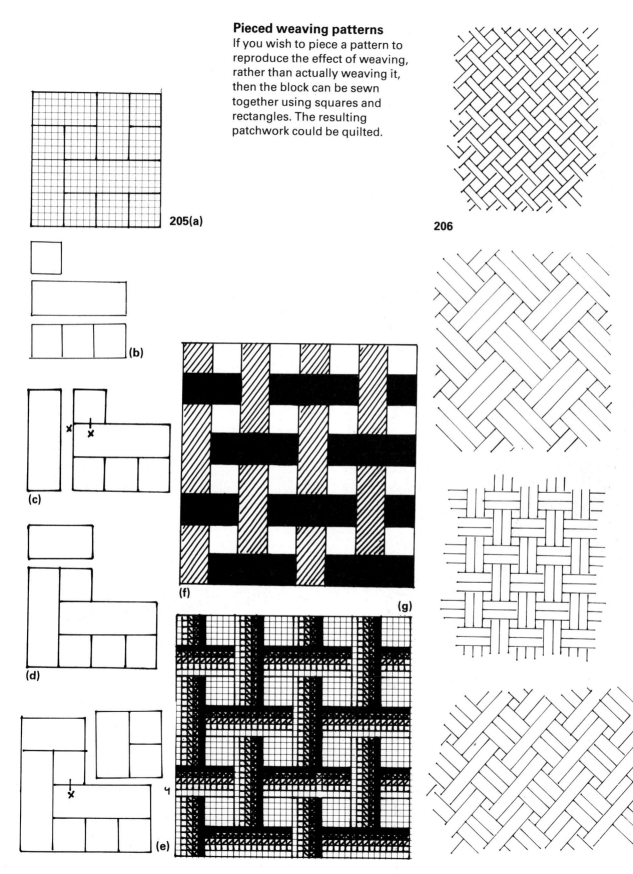

Pieced weaving patterns

If you wish to piece a pattern to reproduce the effect of weaving, rather than actually weaving it, then the block can be sewn together using squares and rectangles. The resulting patchwork could be quilted.

205(a)

206

(b)

(c)

(d)

(e)

(f)

(g)

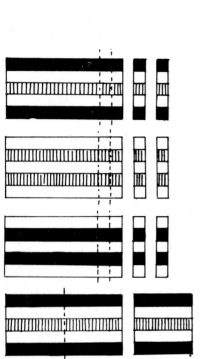

208 A more complicated pattern of squares and stripes. However, when pieced as in the diagram it becomes quite simple

207 A simple strip block which is sewn together in different directions

209 A log cabin block which has been divided to make a pattern resembling a ribbon and buckle. If the colour of the vertical band were red and the horizontal band blue, the cental square could be purple and would give the effect of transparency, with the two colours mixing

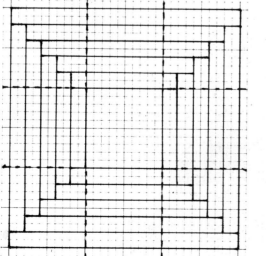

Weaving patterns with diagonal stripes

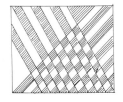

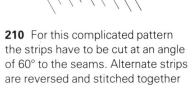

210 For this complicated pattern the strips have to be cut at an angle of 60° to the seams. Alternate strips are reversed and stitched together

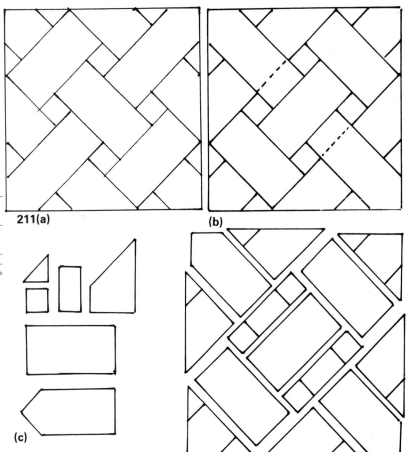

211(a)

(b)

(c)

(d)

211 (a), (b) These patterns have to be pieced according to method 15 because of the spaces between the woven strips. Extra construction lines have been added for machine sewing
(c) The templates required for this pattern
(d) The sewing sequence
(e) The pattern which emerges when four blocks are put together

(e)

212 (a) Cushion which resembles weaving but is in fact pieced. It is made of mattress ticking with applied ribbons, frayed strips and machine and hand embroidery. These were worked as long strips, cut into squares and then stitched together at different angles. White, cream and gold were used to give a warm tone to the fabrics. *(Valerie Campbell-Harding. Ribbons by Offray)*
(b) Detail of the cushion

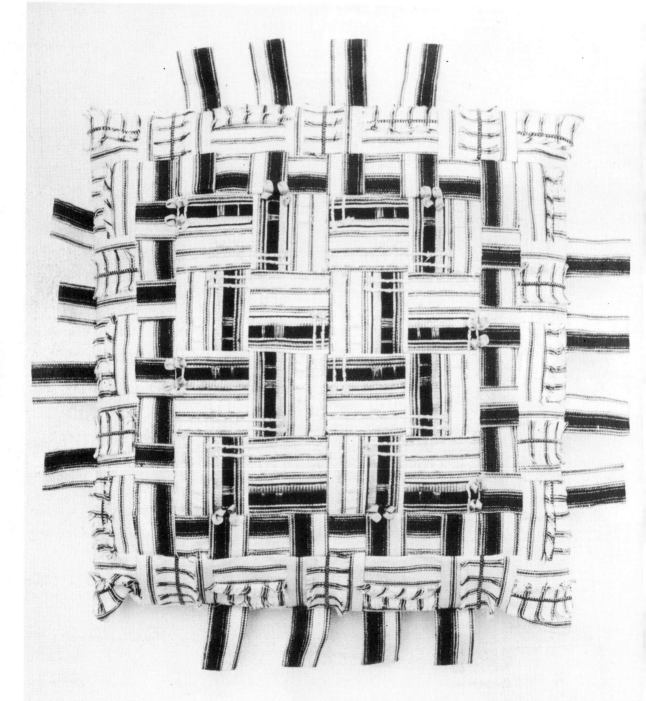

(a)

Plaits and twists

Plaits and twists are the simplest of the interlaced patterns and are not often used by patchworkers. Those shown here can be pieced together using either the machine method 15 (*213-215*), or the hand method 8 (*216-218*) to give the effect of long strips twisted or plaited together, even though the patterns are built up using small pieces. Plaits and twists can be used as borders or all-over patterns. If you are using them as borders, then you will want to turn a corner at some stage. To find the best place to do this, place a small mirror diagonally across the border and slide it backwards and forwards until you find a satisfactory arrangement *(219)*. Draw a line along the bottom of the mirror, trace the pattern up to the line, then turn the tracing paper over and trace the rest of it.

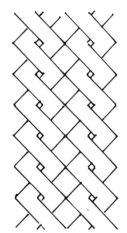

213

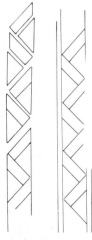 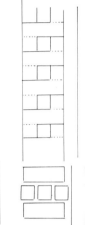 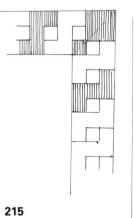 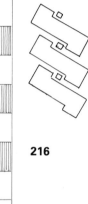

216

215

214

217

 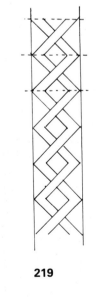

218

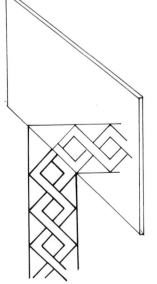

219

Plaited border

To design your own plaited border, plait some yarns or strips of fabric and make a photocopy of them (*220*). Place a piece of graph tracing paper over the top and draw the plaits, making your lines fit the lines of the graph paper. Then fill in the tones – you will need three to make the pattern look like a plait. All the patterns on this page can be pieced by hand (method 8) or machine (method 15).

The pattern shown in figure 222 can be cut using templates and pre-stripped fabric.

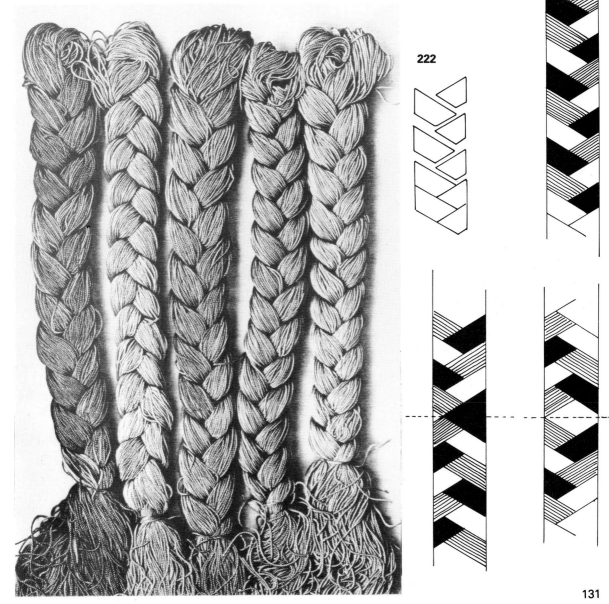

220

221

222

223 Interlaced patterns leaving hexagons and long hexagon shapes between the strips. The first group must be pieced by hand, but the quilt can be machine-pieced

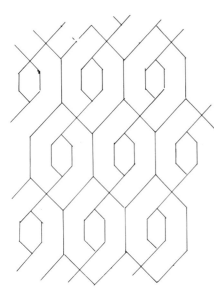

224 Detail of the bed quilt shown in colour plate 4, worked in colours of the spectrum. The colours behind the interlaced pattern graduate from red at the top left-hand corner, through orange, yellow, green and blue to purple at the bottom right corner. The same colours repeat around the border. The darkest tone is black and the strips between are mixed blue and white prints. (*Sheila Wells*)

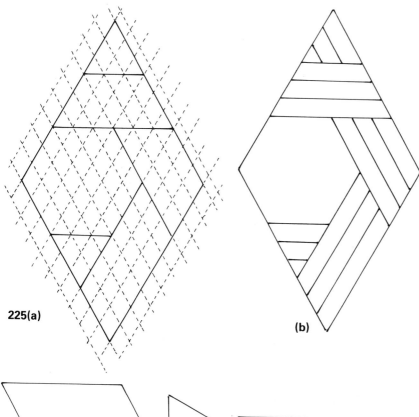

225(a)

(b)

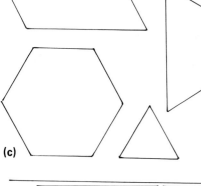

(c)

(d)

(e)

225 (a) The pattern for the quilt was drafted on isometric graph paper (indicated by the dotted lines)
(b) The complete block
(c) The templates needed to make the block
(d), (e) The templates laid on pre-stripped fabric
(f) The sewing sequence. The shapes have to be adapted at the edge of the quilt

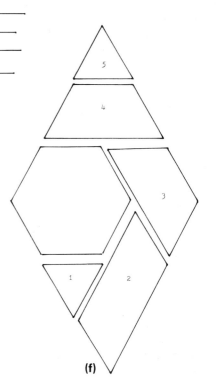

(f)

226-228 Twisted and interlaced patterns which leave negative shapes of hexagons and long hexagons. The patterns on this page can be pieced by machine using method 15 (page 62). They can be drafted on squared paper and used either as all-over or as border patterns

226

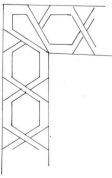

227

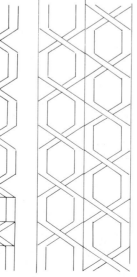

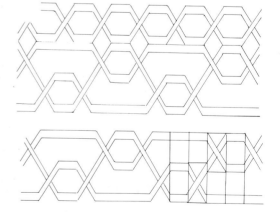

228

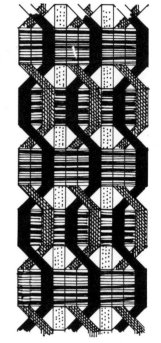

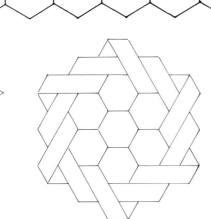

229

229-232 These patterns must be drafted on isometric graph paper with a triangular grid, and the easiest way to piece them would be by hand, using method 8 (page 50). The medallion shapes will fit together to make an all-over pattern, and the others will make either borders or all-over patterns

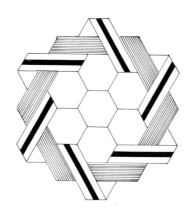

230

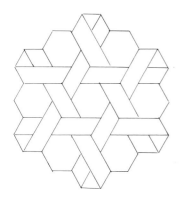

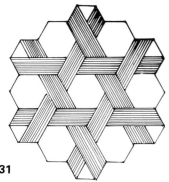

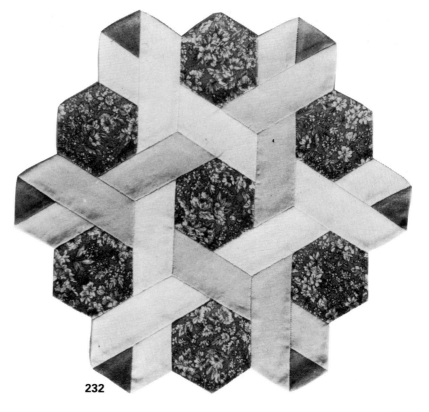

231

232

135

233

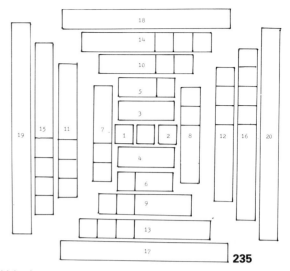

234

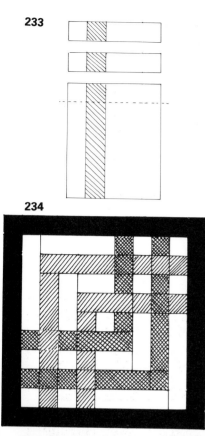

235

Interlaced blocks

The interlaced blocks shown on this page are pieced together by one of the log cabin methods (6 or 7), with some slight changes in the sequence of sewing, as shown in figure 235.

Individual squares and rectangles can be sewn together to make the groups, if only one block is to be made; but if you are going to make a number, long strips of fabric can be sewn together and then cut to make the pieced strips. This will cut the sewing time down considerably and make a large project much less daunting.

237

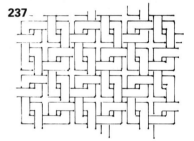

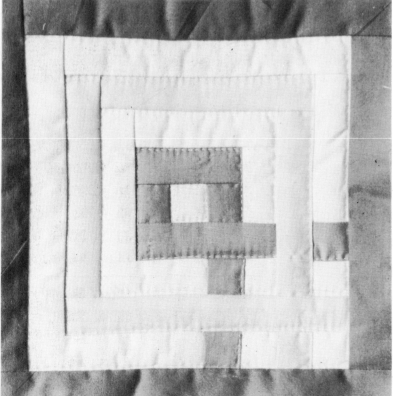

236

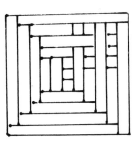

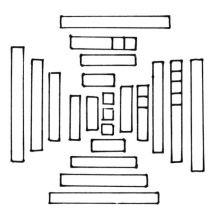

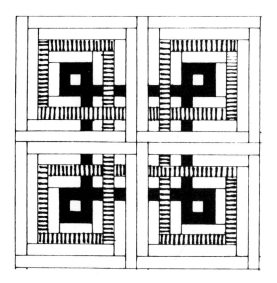

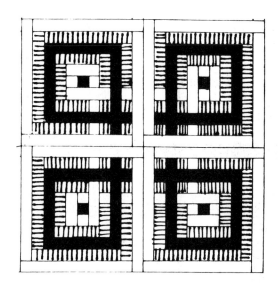

Eight-point star block

An eight-point star block can give interlaced patterns when one or two seam lines are added or left out.

The line drawings on the left show the original block at the top and the subsequent changes. Printed striped fabric or pre-stripped fabric can be used to emphasize the over and under effect. These blocks make good individual patterns for a small area such as a cushion, or can be repeated to make all-over patterns. If you think they are too busy *en masse*, strips of plain fabric can separate the blocks, making a lattice.

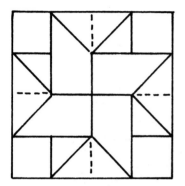

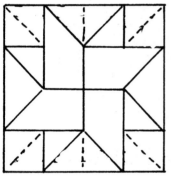

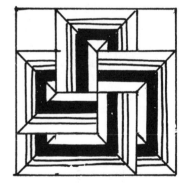

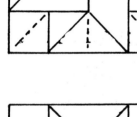
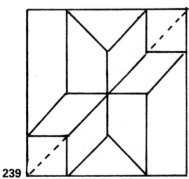

239

240

Design by printing

Designs can be built up using a child's printing set. The wooden printing blocks have linear patterns which all fit in with each other, no matter how they are arranged.

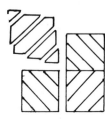
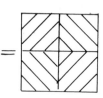
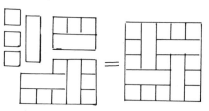

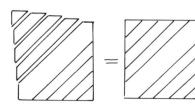

242 *Right* The blocks and their piecing sequences. Two are extremely quick and easy. The second two are not difficult, but are a little fiddly when sewing the outside shapes around the central square. This is best done by sewing half a seam first, then the next three composite shapes to the edges of the square, and finally the rest of the first seam

243 *Below* The completed pattern, with dotted lines showing the position of the four blocks

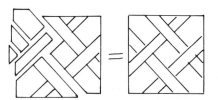

241 The four blocks used in the final pattern shown separately

244 A tracing of the pattern, straightening out some of the kinks left when the printing blocks did not quite join up

245 The final version filled in with dark, medium and light tones. It is easy to take the next step of using colour. Providing the tones are kept the same, the pattern will be similar no matter what colours are used

Bibliography

Albarn, Smith, Steele and Walker, *The Language of Pattern*, Thames and Hudson 1974

Bain, George, *Celtic Art*, Dover 1977

Barclay, Barclay, Gravel, Jacoby, Kohen, Sharp and Touhey, *Seminole Patchwork*, Seminole Research/Design Project

Beyer, Jinny, *The Quilters' Album of Blocks and Borders* , EPM 1980

Boas, Franz, *Primitive Art*, Dover 1962

da Conceicao, Maria, *Finery*, Dover 1979

Dudley, Taimi, *Strip Patchwork*, Van Nostrand Reinhold 1980

Horemis, Spyros, *Optical and Geometrical Patterns and Designs*, Dover 1970

Higgins, Muriel, *New Designs for Machine Patchwork*, Batsford 1980

James, Michael, *The Quiltmaker's Handbook*, Prentice Hall 1978

James, Michael, *The Second Quiltmaker's Handbook*, Prentice Hall 1981

Lancaster, John *Introducing Op Art*, Batsford 1973

Rehmel, Judy, *Key to 1,000 Quilt Patterns*, Rehmel 1978

Rush and Wittman, *The Complete Book of Seminole Patchwork*, Madrona Publishers 1982

Sheets-Dye, Daniel, *Chinese Lattice Design*, Dover 1974

Wade, David, *Geometric Patterns and Borders*, Wildwood House 1982

Suppliers

UK

Dyes

Durham Chemicals Distributors Ltd
55-57 Glengall Road
London SE15 6NQ
Large quantities of Procion M (fibre-reactive) and direct dyes (hot-water)

Candlemakers' Supplies
28 Blythe Road
London W14
Small to medium quantities of Procion M (fibre-reactive) and direct dyes (hot-water)

Yarncraft
112A Westbourne Grove
London W2 5RU
Small to medium quantities of Procion M and direct dyes

Dylon cold- and hot-water dyes are available at most ironmongers, and haberdashery departments of chain stores

Fabrics

The Fabric Studio
10 Frith Street
London W1

McCulloch and Wallis
25-26 Dering Street
London W1

Pongees Ltd
184-186 Old Street
London EC4 9BP
Large quantities only

Strawberry Fayre
Chagford
Newton Abbot
Devon TQ13 8EN

Whaley's (Bradford) Ltd
Harris Court
Great Horton
Bradford
West Yorkshire
BD7 4EQ

H. Wolfin and Son
64 Great Tichfield Street
London W1

All these firms will supply by mail order

USA

Dyes

Dharma Trading Co
P.O. Box 916
San Rafael
California
CA 94902

Farquhar International Ltd
56 Harvester Avenue
Batavia
New York
NY14020

Fabrics

Gutcheon Patchworks
Dept 8
611 Broadway
New York
NY10012

Cabin Fever Calicoes
Box 6256
Washington DC
20015

Index